A NEW ECONOMY

A
NEW
ECONOMY

AN ARGUMENT
FOR ECONOMIC REFORM

F. K. RICHTER

EXPOSITION PRESS
HICKSVILLE, NEW YORK

CONTENTS

PART I
THE
OLD
ECONOMY

1

THE MONETARY SHORTFALL

It has appeared then that, in the ordinary state of society, the master producers and capitalists, though they may have the power, have not the will to consume in the shape of revenue to the necessary extent. And with regard to their workmen, it must be allowed that, if they possessed the will, they have not the power. It is indeed most important to observe that no power of consumption on the part of the laboring classes can ever, according to the common motives which influence mankind, alone furnish an encouragement to the employment of capital.

THOMAS ROBERT MALTHUS
Principles of Political Economy

Do you want to get rich? It's really quite simple. If you want to enrich yourself with knowledge, all you need do is learn more in a given length of time than you forget. If you want to enrich yourself with money, you need only take in more money in a given length of time than you pay out. In both cases, the idea is the same. But the processes are quite different. For instance, you can become richer in knowledge without someone else forgetting anything. In fact, a hundred students, or a million, can sit in their classrooms and become richer in knowledge simultaneously. But you can't take in more *money* than you pay out unless someone else pays out more than he takes in. Putting it another way—and excluding those few who own gold mines—*some people can become richer in money only if others become poorer.* Now, with this obvious proposition in mind, we will examine one of the worst faults in our present economy.

✿　✿　✿

In 1949, a "normal"[1] postwar year, more than 50% of that year's national income of $216 billion was derived from corporate business. This was divided roughly as follows:

Compensation to employees of corporations	$ 88 billion
Taxes paid by corporations	11 billion
Corporate profits after taxes	16 billion
TOTAL	$115 billion

Try to imagine this vast corporate empire combined into a single huge factory: a factory with its own banking and insurance facilities; with its own advertising media and with internal means for supplying itself with raw materials, new plant and equipment. This hypothetical factory will produce all the goods and services that corporations now produce—from canned beans and automobiles to houses, munitions and highway bridges. The owners will be the same industrialists, bankers and businessmen who now own our corporations. Of course, the owners will operate the factory mainly for one purpose: to make a profit Actually, many of these owners of capital already are rich in a monetary way; and some of the profits they receive from the factory will make them richer. Further, even if some of the profits are used to pay for additional plant and equipment, or for research, it is intended that these new facilities later *will* make a profit by returning more than their cost. Owners of capital, you see, build new factories for the same reason they operate the existing ones: to make profits. And these profits, in part, will be accumulated (saved).

Now suppose that the owners of this composite factory pay out to all their workers a total of $90 billion in one year as wages and salaries for doing all the work in the factory (including building new plant and equipment, producing raw materials, advertising and research; and for making all the goods and

---

[1]The years 1947-49 were once used as a base for many postwar economic measurements. However, 1949 is selected mainly because the statistics that year are useful as a simplified example.

services that are to be sold). And suppose that another $10 billion is paid by the factory owners to the government for taxes. Also grant that the owners, in order to make the profit they wish to accumulate, can set the total price for the goods and services to be sold at $115 billion.

If the employees and their government use only their $100 billion income ($90 billion in wages and salaries plus $10 billion in tax revenue) to purchase the factory's goods and services, there will be $15 billion worth left over. That is, 13% of the total output will remain unsold. In this case, since the relatively few owners could not consume very much of the 13% of leftover goods, you can see that the owners would curtail output by about 13% and lay off about 13% of the workers.

But suppose that the employees and the government, after spending their $100 billion current cash income, purchase the remaining $15 billion worth of stuff with credit: $5 billion worth of autos could be bought on the installment plan; $5 billion worth of houses could be bought with mortgages; and $5 billion worth of highways and munitions could be bought with government bonds. Thus, all the goods will be sold ($100 billion cash sales plus $15 billion credit sales). So, everyone will continue to have a job. The $100 billion cash (the original cash purchasing power) can be recycled by the owners to pay wages, salaries and taxes during the next round of business. The owners got the profit they wished to accumulate ($15 billion in interest-bearing bonds, mortgages, notes, etc.). And the workers, together with their government, acquired all the goods and services that were for sale. There is only one flaw in the process: between the act of producing the goods and services, and consuming or acquiring them, there was a slip. The employees who made these things, together with their government, were able to *buy* them only by going into debt by $15 billion in addition to spending all their current income.

Now, let us leave the imaginary factory and return to actual figures. In 1949 (the "normal" postwar year) the total net debt increased by $14.1 billion as follows:

Increase in public debt (federal, state and local)	$ 4.0	billion
Increase in private mortgage debt	5.8	billion
Increase in private non-mortgage debt	4.1	billion
Increase in corporate debt	0.2	billion
TOTAL	$14.1	billion

This, then, is the monetary shortfall. Each year of relatively high prosperity, there is a big increase in the total debt that is owed. This is necessary because those who own the capital and employ labor insist upon taking in more money than they pay out. The general run of people, together with their governments (federal, state and local), make this possible by paying out more than they take in (by going into debt, that is). Except during depressions there is always this slip between the cup and the lip.

And the depressions? They occur whenever the general run of people, together with their various governments, stop going deeper into debt. When this happens, a portion of the goods and services produced under the auspices of the owners of capital remains unsold. With unsold goods on hand, the owners cut back production. So, layoffs and shutdowns start, then spread. During the ensuing depression, with unemployment increasing and the level of business declining, many workers and small businesses become the victims of bankruptcy or foreclosure.

*   *   *

Of course, the argument thus far is highly simplified and omits many of the complications. But it is not an oversimplification. At the heart of our highly complex economy, there is a simple mathematical defect: for every $10 of purchasing fuel required to keep the economic machine running, only $9 worth of cash purchasing power is produced. This deficit—that is, the required monetary input less the cash purchasing power output—is the monetary shortfall. The latter, defined with practical precision, is the portion of total current sales that is paid for with obligations against expected future income. Of course, such obligations are mostly interest-bearing debts. So, it turns out that it is debt that keeps the economic machine running. If the total debt fails to increase fast enough, the economic machine slows down. As simple as that. Worse yet, there is always the danger of a terrible crunch, like 1929-39.

Now, there is a way to graphically portray the economy going through that crunch and, at the same time, justify our use of a hypothetical "composite factory." For example, the level of factory employment provides a reasonable measure of the total level of output and is quite similar, conceptually, to our assumed single huge factory. Also the annual change in net debt is a very good measure of the total monetary shortfall for the year.

In Figure 1, the index of factory employment and the annual increases of debt are plotted for the 25-year period of 1920 through 1945. Note that the correlation between employment and the rate of increase of debt is shown very clearly. In the quarter century covered by the graph, the total net debt grew from $135 billion in 1920 to $407 billion in 1945. This is an increase of $272 billion, or an average of over $10 billion a year for the 25 years. During this period, the annual monetary shortfall varied from $0.4 billion in 1921 and 1930 (both depressions) to $57.3 billion in 1944 (the war boom). During the depth of the great depression, 1931-33, cancellation of debts through foreclosures, bankruptcies, forced sales, etc., was so great that the total net debt was reduced by about $22 billion.

The line graphs in Figure 1 do more than show that factory employment and annual changes in the net debt rise and fall together. Those lines demonstrate the basic proposition that the level of economic prosperity depends upon the rate at which debt is increasing. At three points—1921, 1930, 1938—they show that when there is no increase in debt, there is depression. This remarkable correlation of factory employment and expansion of debt confirms the basic argument. No counterargument, however many complications are introduced, can erase this simple stark reality.

Since the great depression of 1929-39, there has been no terrible crunch. There has been, however, a pronounced escalation in the annual rate of shortfall. This, of course, is understandable.

FIGURE 1

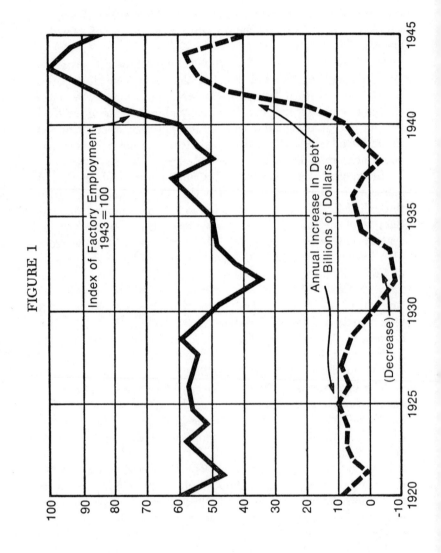

If the total debt is expanded year after year with some increase in the *rate* of expansion as time goes on, prosperity is maintained.

The historical record of the monetary shortfall since 1946 is shown in Table 1-1. It shows that the total debt owed increased sevenfold from 1946 through 1974. Each year for over 28 years, some *additional* expected future income was obligated to pay for part of the purchases made that year. The monetary shortfall varied from a low of $15 billion in 1949 (7% of national income) to a high of $262 billion in 1973 (25% of national income). By the end of 1975 the total net debt amounted to nearly $3 trillion.

As can be seen in the table the total net debt did not grow at a constant rate. The *growth* of total debt proceeded inexorably, but the *rate* of increase rose and fell. And with each slowdown in the rate of growth there was economic recession.

These recessions occurred in 1949, 1954, 1960-61, 1970, and 1974-75 (determined in each case by the increased unemployment). Then with each subsequent boost in the rate of debt-growth the preceding recession was temporarily cured. However, whenever the slug of debt-medicine aimed at curing the recession was a bit overdone there was a side effect: inflation. The inflationary periods came in 1950, 1955, and 1965-75. The latter period of inflation began slowly with a 2% price rise in 1965 increasing to a 5% rise in 1968, but rising to a 12% inflation rate for 1974. Efforts at price controls in the early seventies did not stop the inflation.

Actually, the reader can learn much about this purchasing-power defect in the existing economy from the graph and Table 1-1. For example, the table shows that by the end of 1963 over one trillion dollars of expected future earnings had been obligated to pay for past purchases. By the end of 1971, the obligated amount was two trillion dollars. Some time during 1976 it will have reached three trillion.

The remainder of the chapter will be devoted to examining some of the complications omitted in the preceding simplified explanation.

✻   ✻   ✻

Table 1-1

NET PUBLIC AND PRIVATE DEBT, 1946-74
(*In Billions of Dollars*)

Year	End of Year Total*	Debt Increase (Monetary Shortfall)
1946	397	
1947	416	19
1948	431	15
1949	446	15—Recession
1950	486	40
1951	519	33
1952	550	31
1953	582	32
1954	606	24—Recession
1955	665	59
1956	698	33
1957	728	30
1958	769	41
1959	831	62
1960	872	41—Recession
1961	930	58
1962	997	67
1963	1,072	75
1964	1,154	82
1965	1,246	92
1966	1,340	95
1967	1,440	100
1968	1,582	143
1969	1,735	153
1970	1,868	133—Recession
1971	2,046	178
1972	2,283	237
1973	2,545	262
1974	2,777	232—Recession begins

*Source: *Survey of Current Business,* May 1969, May 1973, June 1974.

THE ACQUISITORS

The simplified explanation implied that all of the monetary shortfall (in the form of interest-bearing debt instruments) ends up in the hands of the owners of corporations. In the example year, 1949, this amounted to $14 billion. Actually, not all of that $14 billion was accumulated by the owners of corporations. Anyone—entertainer, trader, speculator, farmer, politician, rack-eteer—who took in more money than he paid out acquired some of the debt instruments that other people owed.

Consider a movie star who was paid a million dollars during the year. Whatever portion of this he "saved" in monetary in-struments (bonds, etc.) came from the pool of expanding debt. Note, however, that the film company that paid the star a million *was* a corporation and expected to get back *more* than the million. Also, a politician who took a large bribe and hid it away in his safe deposit box, was simply being employed by one or more businesslike corporations that expected to make a profit on the transaction. Even so deserving a man as the old farmer who sold his farm on the edge of the city for one million dollars is paid by a development corporation which, after divid-ing the farm into small lots, sells it for $5 million.

So, around the periphery of the corporate estate, there are those individuals—clever, lucky, deserving, frugal or crooked—who take in more money than they pay out. Thus, they acquire monetary riches. But they do not necessarily *insist* upon this as their price for producing. Doctors, actors, farmers, politicians, even gangsters, would ply their trades just to earn a good living. Not so the industrial, commercial and financial corporations. They are in business to make money. For many reasons, they are in a better position to make large sums available for their owners' private acquisition. In addition, they are quick to lay off workers and curtail production if the increase in debt is inadequate and some goods, therefore, are left unsold. So, factory employment (factories being mainly corporate-owned) follows very sensi-tively the rate at which debt is increasing. This is why the graphs in Figure 1 portrayed such a revealing picture of our defective economy.

MONEY

The simplest definition, or concept, of money is legal tender (currency plus coin or, commonly, cash). Even at this simple conceptual level, however, money introduces a small complication into the monetary shortfall.

The economy prices its goods about 7% to 20% higher than the effective monetary purchasing power it generates. This deficit in generated purchasing power is the monetary shortfall. Since the deficit is made up, or overcome, by borrowing, the annual short- fall is defined as that portion of current production purchased with obligations against future income; and we use the annual increase in net public and private debt to quantify the shortfall.

But the federal government disturbs this simplicity by gen- erating some effective monetary purchasing power on its own: by printing it. Each year, because of the growth in population, business activity, prices, etc., the government increases the supply of currency in circulation. The increase, of course, helps to over- come some of the shortfall. From 1960 through 1974 currency in circulation increased from $33 billion to $69 billion. So, in 14 years, $36 billion of shortfall was overcome. But in the same period the net debt overcame more than 98% of the shortfall; new currency less than 2%. By ignoring the 2% we can return to the simple relationship: the monetary shortfall is measured by the increase in net debt.

FUNNY MONEY

Economists and bankers are not much impressed by simple money. Knowing that most monetary transactions are by check they concern themselves with the "total money supply," which they call "M1." This is measured by total demand deposits (checking accounts) plus the currency outside the vaults of banks and the Treasury.

Others think that bank savings accounts also act like money and add this, calling the result "M2." Still others think that deposits in mutual savings banks and savings and loan associations should be added in, too, and they call this "M3."

As of January 1975 the total of these various concepts of money looked like this:

Legal tender money (currency)	M0——$ 70 billion
Currency plus checkbook money	M1——$282 billion
Money as measured by	M2——$616 billion
Money as measured by	M3——$988 billion

Obviously, as one gets higher in the M's, there is money all over the place. The secret is that all the "money" beyond M0 is balanced by debt: it is the plus, or asset, side of a negative or debt instrument. This is explained more fully in Chapter 2. Suffice it to say here that this supermoney introduces no error in the measurement of the shortfall: it is *part* of the monetary shortfall.

EQUITIES

There *is* a "stock market" and some people get rich in it. Others, of course, get poor in it. But these trading operations have little effect on the monetary shortfall. For example, these stock-trading tycoons would accomplish as much and have about the same effect if they went to a quiet place and played high-stakes poker.

Common and preferred stocks represent ownership of corporate assets. They are not debt and they do not bear interest. So, they are not added into the measurement of the monetary shortfall.

However, in connection with the growth of monopolistic and conglomerate corporations, equities of some smaller corporations are exchanged for debt instruments of a larger company as the smaller is absorbed into the giant. Here there is a replacement of equity by debt which introduces a potentially significant error into the *measurement* of the shortfall (i.e., net debt). But this is in the opposite direction of an error created by the exchange of convertible bonds into equities. Further compensating effects are introduced by "supermoney" (see Adam Smith's book *Supermoney*). In this trick, the tycoon runs up the market price of his stock shares, then peels off some and spends them; money, M10, maybe.

All this Byzantine maneuvering by these amalgamating tycoons obviously is inimical to measuring the monetary shortfall with ease and precision. So, those who do so much in creating the monetary shortfall also make it more difficult to measure.

CORPORATE DEBT

When a corporation obligates some expected future income to buy some of the current output (for raw materials, new construction, etc.), the resulting debt adds to the measurement of the monetary shortfall. Well it should; for this corporate debt *is* covering some of the shortfall and, thereby, eases the debt burden on individuals and governments. That is, an expanding corporate debt will result in employment which otherwise might have to be supported by unbalanced public budgets or accepted as unemployment.

The expansion of corporate debt, however, is a sometime thing, as explained more fully in Chapter 2. Obviously, corporations are not in business to pay out more than they take in over the long run. Thus, in the simplified explanation, the sample year, 1949, was selected not to evade corporate debt but to avoid a complication that is special rather than general.

In times of increasing prosperity the expansion of corporate debt becomes a substantial part of the annual increase in net debt. The tax laws stimulate this expansion because earnings applied to debt-interest are tax deductible, while earnings accruing to stockholders are taxable. For utilities, airlines, railroads, etc., there is an additional incentive to favor debt financing over equity financing: the former enhances the earnings for the equity holders.

One minor component of net corporate debt, however, does

introduce a small error into the measurement of the monetary shortfall: finance corporation debt. Finance corporations issue bonds and notes that add to the total corporate debt. The proceeds of this borrowing are then lent to consumers, thus adding to private individual debt. So it is measured twice in the total net debt. Thus, two dollars of debt are created to overcome one dollar of the monetary shortfall. Finance corporation debt, however, is only about 2% of the total net debt. The error it causes is almost exactly cancelled by the 2% error in the other direction caused by newly printed currency.

OFFICIAL MEASUREMENT OF THE NET DEBT

About 5 months after the end of each calendar year the U.S. Department of Commerce, unaware that it is measuring the monetary shortfall, promulgates its estimate of the net total of public and private debt as of the end of the preceding year.

While most big creditors such as banks and insurance companies are meticulous in their accounting of the monies owed them, the government has no easy time assembling the total of all debts. In fact, the estimate is compiled with the use of assumptions, blowups, geometric interpolations, cross tabulations, ratio multipliers and extrapolations. The resulting net error may be cumulative or offsetting to the error created by the conglomerating tycoons churning their stocks and bonds in frenzied illusion. More likely, since the total monetary shortfall now reaches into the trillions of dollars, such errors are of only minor significance.

And so, without further nit-picking, we shall hereafter consider that the annual monetary shortfall is roughly equal to, and is measured by, the annual increase in the net public and private debt.

THE LIMITS TO DEBT

In 1916 net public and private debt totaled about $80 billion; in 1976 it was $3,000 billion. From this one might think it could grow forever—except that once, in 1930, it did stop growing. When the debt-growth stopped so did a major part of the American economy; and the resulting depression lasted ten long years.

Since the experience of financing World War II (it was won with a few tons of high-grade paper printed up into government bonds) the idea of using public debt to stimulate economic expansion has become more widely acceptable. With the increase throughout the government of men familiar with Keynesian economics the use of federal debt ("fiscal policy" it's called) to keep us out of depressions became an unstated public policy, and the operation of it has often been cleverly managed. Along the way, awareness dawned that a rising price index had the effect of eroding the burden of past debts. We could borrow a billion dollars and, after a few years of creeping inflation, discover that the old billion we owed was only owed in 50¢ dollars. Thus "a little bit of inflation is a good thing" became the conventional wisdom. The hope that the growth of debt and, along with it, prosperity, might go on forever remained alive.

Unfortunately, a large part of the burden of old debt is the interest on it. And the rate of interest tends to creep up along with the creeping inflation. So when old debts are refunded the interest costs are often higher than before. Besides in new borrowing one had to borrow twice as many 50¢ dollars to accomplish what half as many $1.00 dollars had done before. Thus the fun part of inflation is, to say the least, somewhat moderated.

While none can say how high the federal debt can go, there are good reasons to believe that most other debtors are subject to some restraint, among them the following:

1. Individuals go into debt with some expectations of eventually paying it off. Sooner or later they will try.

2. As debts increase the possibility of bankruptcy or foreclosure arises. Most individuals have an innate dislike for failure; and corporations, even cities, are managed by individuals.

3. Lenders can become reluctant to extend more credit to those who continue to get deeper into debt. Of course, the lender then might merely lend his funds elsewhere. But he does have an

alternative: retain his lendable funds and increase his own liquidity.

4. As debts increase so does the interest cost. Even the federal government can't escape this.

5. It is at least mathematically possible for the rising interest costs to press hard upon the debtor's total income.

Enough. This does not establish the limit to debt or prove beyond doubt that there is a limit. Chapter 2, perhaps, will do the latter. Even so, these reasons undermine the hope of infinite elasticity and make it manifest that the stoppage of the increase in debt in 1930 was not just an unlucky accident.

2

SUNDRY OBSERVATIONS
ON THE NATURE OF DEBT

> For about a century we have been living in a society
> that is not even the society of money but that of the ab-
> stract symbols of money. . . . A society founded on signs
> is, in its essence, an artificial society in which man's
> physical truth is handled as something artificial.
>
> ALBERT CAMUS
> *University of Uppsala, 1957*

Americans must be very fond of debt—we have created so
much of it. At the beginning of 1975, the net debt, public and
private, totaled about $2,780 billion. At that same time our stock
of currency amounted to about $68 billion. So, plainly, we
legally owed more than forty times as much legal money as there
was. Or, if you prefer to be old-fashioned and think in terms of
gold, of which there was about $12 billion on hand, we owed
over two hundred times as much as there was. In either event,
being beyond the point of owing only a *little* more legal money
than we have, the number of times more becomes a matter only
of degree. That is, one becomes insolvent by owing more than
one has; to owe forty times as much simply makes it more
emphatic.

Nor is the process of gaining such heights of insolvency very
complicated. For an analogy, consider this: five poker players,
of whom one is a consistent winner, can enter a room, lock the
door and play poker indefinitely. They can do this even though
each player has only a small amount of cash—provided, of course,
that the winner accepts the IOUs of the losers. Let us assume that
each player enters the room with $100 in cash. Once the con-

sistent winner has the $500 in his hands, all of his further win-
nings must be in the form of IOUs; that is, debt. When the game
finally is stopped—either because the losers refuse to sign more
IOUs or the winner refuses to accept more—and an attempt is
made to "settle up," the need for more cash obviously will be
acute. And the need will be acute whether the consistent winner
has won $10,000 or only $1,000.

In the previous chapter we saw that it is an expanding internal
debt that produces prosperity, just as a free flow of IOUs keeps
the poker game going full tilt. The purpose of this chapter is to
explore more fully the reasons for this, and to examine some other
little-known aspects of the nature of debt. It would be well to
do this without too many digressions. So, we shall dispose of
some side issues first, so to avoid distractions later.

MONEY

In the broad sense, *money* is anything that people consider
it to be. Seashells, beaver pelts, cows, even cigarettes have
served as money. Rare metals such as gold and silver have the
longest history of use. When made into coins by a trustworthy
government these metals became money in the precise sense:
acceptable in the settlement of all debts, and so decreed by law.
This is the definition of legal tender. Nowadays, gold and silver
are more useful as commercial metals, just like platinum and
tungsten, than as monetary metals. For this reason, and others,
paper currency has become the main form of legal tender—
that is, cash, or money in the precise sense. You will note that
our poker game started out using such money. Each loser
switched to IOUs only after he had lost all his cash. But this
switch required a decision by the losers to go into debt; and by
the winner, to accept credit. The IOUs are "monetary" in the
sense that they are promises to pay some amount of money. But
the winner wasn't legally required to accept them. So, the IOUs
are debt, not money. As debt, they are analogous to notes, mortgages, bonds and checks. These latter are not cash, merely a
promise to pay cash later.

MOTIVES

As to motives, there is little to gain from assuming them to be highly complex. The poker players, for example, are having fun. The losers are buying fun willingly, just as they would buy fancy cars, vacations or TV sets. They are unwilling to stop buying when their cash assets are spent: they go into debt rather than forgo their fun. So, the one economic product of the poker game—a consumer's good (fun)—is analogous to all such goods and services in the economy: from dinners charged on credit cards to warplanes bought with government bonds.

The winner is having fun making money. Motive enough. Nor will he stop just because he has cornered the money supply. He will lend it back to his customers in exchange for their IOUs, and have the fun of winning it all over again. This he considers better than shutting down the game. But he looks upon the IOUs not as money but as claims to money in the future.

Superficially, the consistent winner appears analogous to the quick-money artists in our economy: the traders, speculators, racketeers, entertainers, etc. Such people seem to get rich without adding anything very solid to our economy. But one of these chaps well might continue the game without the IOUs—just for the fun of it. Our richest crooners, in other circumstances, quite likely would sing for their suppers. But our consistent winner is made of different stuff: his customers must pay with money, sign a promise to pay money, or get out of the game. He is playing for keeps, not funsies. So he is analogous to the owners of capital.

SAVINGS

In modern economics, "savings" and "investment" have nearly identical meaning. "Investment" is production that is not consumed; "savings" is income that is not consumed. Keynes wrote that "they are necessarily equal in amount, being, for the community as a whole, merely different aspects of the same thing." Our poker game produces only one thing: fun. And it is immediately consumed. Obviously, then, this game produces no savings. When the game started, assets were $500 in currency, divided equally among the players, plus the value of cards, chips, table and chairs, owned, let us say, by the consistent winner. In due time, the winner finds he has $500 in cash, $5,000 in IOUs, and the original equipment. He has acquired savings of $5,000 in monetary assets. But the losers have acquired $5,000 in monetary liabilities. For the group as a whole, proper accounting (deduction of liabilities from assets) will show there to have been no net addition to savings. So, the winner's hoard of IOUs is not really "savings," nor is it really "money"; it is merely a pecuniary accumulation. Hereafter, however, we will call such things "monetary savings," anyway.

CAPITAL

Capital is a special sort of savings (investment): goods or assets used for the production of other goods and assets. In the poker game the cards, table and chairs are capital; so, too, is the winner's currency, all these things being used in the production of fun for the consumers and profits for the owner. Further, with the game going well, the winner might invest (save) some of his winnings in new capital by paying the losers to build a new chair. This can prove to be a great idea; a new customer can be seated in the game; the money paid out can be won back again; the chair itself is pleasing and its value can be posted to the accounts as new capital (investment) (savings). Indeed the winner can become quite enthusiastic about new chairs. This new capital can be symbolized by printed shares of stock which can be used as chips in another game: the stock market. The chairs (and the equivalent shares of stock) are fine things so long as they bring new players into the game and more IOUs to the winner. There's the crux: the business of business is to make "money." The owner of capital feels the better the more capital (or shares) he owns. But the reason he feels better is that the more capital he owns the more "money" he expects to get.

We return to the subject matter.

DEBT IS THE STUFF
MONETARY SAVINGS ARE MADE OF

In the poker game you can see that, except for a small amount of cash, the consistent winner accumulates winnings only because the other players are going into debt. It works much the same way in our economic system. The consistent winners (whether speculators or owners of capital) acquire monetary savings only because the general run of people and their governments (federal, state and local) go into debt. Moreover, the game of accumulation in our real-life economy is played with a relatively constant amount of currency—just as it is in the poker game. In the six-year postwar boom period from mid-1946 to mid-1952, currency in circulation remained at $28 billion, plus or minus only 4%. During these same years our real-life IOUs—net debt, that is—increased by more than $150 billion.

Of course, all this is brought about by processes more intricate than the simple arrangement of financial matters in a poker game. Besides, in our real-life economy, the winners—the owners of capital, that is—complicate things a bit by returning a part of their winnings to the stream of business in the form of investment. "The process of putting earnings back into the business," wrote Professor Taussig of Harvard, "does mean that great efficient establishments are enlarged. . . . But the eventual outcome is the emergence of a fortune. . . . Eventually the owners do get the benefit of their earnings. . . . the melon is cut."

In any given year, some businesses are expanding while others are cutting melons. Let us, simply for illustration, consider a group of businesses large enough to have total sales of $200 billion in one year. Now assume that 10% ($20 billion) of this is net profit after taxes. It would be quite realistic for half ($10 billion) of this annual profit to be reinvested; the other half ($10 billion) ending up as the year's monetary savings. Since net profit on the $200 billion sales is 10%, the total expenditure of our assumed group for wages, salaries and taxes (in producing and marketing their goods) amounts to $180 billion (i.e., 90% of 200 = 180). And if half of the net profit is used for investment, another $10 billion will have been paid out for wages, salaries, taxes, etc., largely for the production of new plant and equipment. Thus the business group that takes in $200 billion each year from all sources pays out only $190 billion. Some may view this as plain Yankee cleverness. Clever though it is, it must be apparent that taking in $200 billion and paying out only $190 billion would exhaust the total supply of legal money (i.e., currency) in only a few years. But the supply of currency stays fairly constant. So, it should be obvious that the portion of profit used for monetary savings is not taken out of the legal money supply.

Next, consider the people (and their governments) who received the $190 billion in wages, salaries, taxes, etc., that the business group paid out. They are the ones who bought the $200 billion of goods and services that constitute the annual sales of the business group. Of course the people couldn't *pay* for it all, because their income was only $190 billion. So, they had to go into debt $10 billion in addition to spending all their current income for the year. This debt is mainly in the form of bank loans, charge accounts, installment credit, mortgages and public bonds. Note that the cash part of the total sales is equal to the purchasing power paid out by the business group in the first place. Thus the business group gets its money back, and uses it to continue its activities. The debt part of the sales is really the part that sooner or later is *accumulated* by the melon cutters. *Debt, then, makes the accumulation of fortunes possible.*

At this point it should be fairly evident that profits used for accumulation (as distinguished from those used for investment) are not gained through plain Yankee cleverness. Rather, they result from the gullibility of the general run of people (and their governments) who spend more than their incomes. The owners of capital may set a price for their goods high enough to include a profit intended for accumulation; but for them to sell the goods at this price and actually accumulate the profit, the buyers must agree to go into debt to buy them. That is, the incurring of the debt by the debtors must *precede* its accumulation by the acquisitors.

It is certainly obvious that money owed (i.e., a debt) must be owed to (saved by) someone; and that a bond issued must, therefore, be held. For example, government savings bonds are a popular form of liquid savings on the one hand, and a form of public debt on the other. Cash reserves in insurance and pension funds will be found, upon investigation, to be held in the form of public or corporate bonds, most generally.

But it is not quite so obvious that a loan made at the bank will permit someone else to make a deposit of the same amount, and that the total bank deposits of the nation can be increased only by prior borrowing. Perhaps we all understand, when we make a deposit at the bank, that the banker will lend it at the first opportunity. But we seldom realize that our deposit is made possible in the first place only by someone else drawing down his deposit or, if our deposit is a new addition to total deposits, someone else must have borrowed at a bank just previously.

An explanation of modern banking practice may be of interest. Almost always there are excess reserves (money available to make loans) somewhere within the banking system. The government sets the rate for legal reserves and, upon occasion, will reduce reserve requirements if the banking system seems to be running out of money to lend. The rate also varies on different types of deposits, and for different parts of the country. For a realistic figure we can use 10% as a rough average on an overall basis. This means that, for each $100 that comes into the banking system as a deposit, $90 may be lent out.

For simplicity, we will ignore the excess reserves for the moment and consider a potential depositor, "Abe," who has come by $1,000 in *new* money. Let's say he just dug up $1,000 worth of gold. After exchanging the gold for new currency, Abe will deposit his $1,000 *somewhere* in the banking system. This will increase aggregate deposits by $1,000. And, by law, the banking system may lend out $900 of this new deposit, keeping $100 (10%, that is) as the required reserve.

As soon as Abe's deposit is made, the banker is put under strong pressure to lend it out. Banks gain profits by making loans. So, the bank's owners will be anxious to lend out the full legal amount. The people who want to borrow—for purchasing a house, or car, or for business purposes—are persistent in pressing the banker for the loan. So, you may be sure the banker will lend the full $900, to "Ben," let us say.

Now, Ben borrows only so he can spend. That is, he wouldn't borrow just to hoard; and relending to another would make Ben himself a banker. So, Ben purchases a house, for example, from a builder, "Cal." Builder Cal deposits the money in some bank within the banking system, which promptly lends out 90% of it to "Dan." Dan buys something from "Ed." And Ed makes a deposit. The process continues along these lines—according to the accompanying tabulation, where the transactions are listed alphabetically in their order of occurrence—until the original $1,000 has been lent out and redeposited ten times.

		New Deposits				New Loans
Abe's original deposit		$ 1,000	Ben's borrowing			$ 900
Cal's desposit		900	Dan's	"		810
Ed's	"	810	F	"		730
G	"	730	H	"		655
I	"	655	J	"		590
K	"	590	L	"		530
M	"	530	N	"		470
		and so on				and so on
	Ultimate Total	$10,000				$9,000

It will be seen from the tabulation that, except for Abe's original deposit, all subsequent deposits depend upon there being a prior loan. In actual practice, since new gold is such rare stuff, Abe would normally have acquired the $1,000 from someone else who had borrowed it from the pool of existing excess reserves, thereby increasing loans by $1,000 and bringing the two totals equal at $10,000. So, it should be quite evident that almost every new addition to total bank deposits is dependent on there being an *equal and prior loan*. Debt, then, is the stuff bank deposits are made of.

Mathematically, this hocus-pocus expansion of "checkbook

money" is fairly straightforward. But some aspects of the process are obscured from the individual participants. A loan made at one bank usually ends up being deposited in another. Though they are both in the same banking system, there is no easy way for the second banker, or his new depositor, to learn that the money being deposited has been borrowed just recently by another person from another bank. Besides, it is difficult for the banker, whose accounting system tells him that 100% of the money he owes his depositors is balanced precisely by 10% in money reserves and 90% in loans, to realize that 100% minus 100% can't be made to equal zero in this case because the depositors and borrowers are *different people.* Van Morganpont's deposits and Joe Doake's debts cancel out only in the minds of accountants and bankers, not in real life.

So, except for very small amounts of gold, if the government is not printing additional currency and if hoarded currency is stable, it is possible for there to be net additions to the total bank deposits of the nation only if there have been equal prior borrowings from the banking system. And if economic activity is fairly stable, too, so that there is no short-run need for additional currency in circulation, the act of borrowing by the debtors makes it almost necessary for the accumulators to deposit an equal amount to their accounts; for the acquisitive won't want the excess cash lying around their premises.

THE INDUCEMENT TO INVEST
DEPENDS UPON EXPANDING DEBT

In considering another side of the nature of debt it is important to remember that, for all practical purposes, an increase in personal monetary savings must be preceded by an equal increase in internal debt. Of course, the increase in currency supply can add a little something to fortunes without a corresponding increase in debt. From 1950 through 1970, the currency supply grew by $27 billion but debt increased by $1,360 billion. So, on the average, the addition to fortunes was 2% cash, 98% credit. Newly mined gold is even less significant, averaging around .05% of the debt increase. Monetary assets gained from abroad, through favorable trade balance, etc., would add to domestic fortunes without an increase in domestic debt. But this can cut both ways; indeed, from 1945 through 1975 the net effect of foreign trade has been a *loss* of monetary assets. So, except for these temporary or minor devices, our domestic fortunes must be born, and raised, by our domestic debt.

Such being the case, the problem of searching existing statistical data for annual changes in monetary savings can be bypassed. You see, we can use the analogous changes in net debt. These data are readily available. And note that, in doing this, the change in *total* monetary savings, including those in personal holding corporations, etc., will be counted. This is the method used to prepare Table 2-1, in which annual expenditures for new plant and equipment are listed for comparison with annual changes in total pecuniary accumulations (measured by changes in net debt).

Table 2-1

Date	Expenditures on New Plant and Equipment		Pecuniary Accumulation (Increase in Net Debt)
1970	$ 80	billion	$ 133 billion
1971	81	"	177 "
1972	88	"	224 "
1973	100	"	260 "
1974	112	"	230 "
Total	$461.0	billion	$1024 billion
5-year average	92	billion	205 billion

The purpose of this table will be made clear a little later on. But first, let us review—in a brief and simplified way—some modern economic theory. According to Keynes,[1] a high rate of employment is dependent upon a high rate of investment; and the rate of investment is dependent upon the "inducement to

---

[1] *The General Theory of Employment, Interest and Money* (New York: Harcourt Brace & Co.).

invest." The intensity of this inducement to invest is measured by the difference between the going rate of interest and the *expected* rate of net return on new capital (this latter called, by Keynes, "the marginal efficiency of capital"). In other words, if the interest rate is 6% and an investor *thinks* that the next piece of new capital will yield a net return over all expenses at a rate of 10%, then the rate, or intensity, of the inducement to invest is 4%. So, in such a case, an investor might gain an extra 4% by putting his money in new capital rather than lending (i.e., accumulating) it. Of course, the investor doesn't actually *know* what rate the new capital will return over its period of life until it is determined later by actual experience.

It will be noted that Keynes implies, in this theory, a basic assumption that the investor is interested primarily in the *return* on his investment. The reader will agree, no doubt, that this is a reasonable assumption. In other words, investment is a means to future monetary savings.

But the reader should recognize that these future accumulations which the investor *thinks* he will receive as the return on his new capital will not be forthcoming unless internal debt is expanding throughout the period of life of the new investment. Since we know that people will not continue indefinitely to go deeper into debt, it is obvious that, over the long run, the investor will face a period when his capital will not produce the profit returns he *thought* it would.

However, at the time the decision is made to go ahead with the investment (which creates employment and promotes prosperity), this future difficulty as to returns does not control the matter. Rather, the investor bases his judgment of the expected rate of return from new capital on the conditions that prevail at the time of his decision. In other words, if the potential investor can see that his *existing* capital is making money for him, he will presume that additional capital will do likewise.

Glancing back now at Table 2-1 it will be seen that in those boom years enough debt was provided for a thumping increase in annual monetary savings. And side by side with these fortunes being made are generous expenditures for investment for the purpose of bringing in more and bigger fortunes. The sight and knowledge of fortunes actually being made encourage the owners of capital to try to make more. *Nothing, then, of a psychological nature could be more favorable to the inducement to invest than that there be increasing debt* (i.e., fortunes actually being made). *And nothing of a psychological nature could have a more unfavorable effect upon the inducement to invest than that there be no increase in debt* (i.e., no fortunes being made).

So much, then, for the psychological aspects of the inducement to invest. But there remains the problem of what happens to this inducement when, in actuality, debt fails to expand; and, as a necessary consequence, existing capital fails to return a profit suitable for accumulation. This will be discussed more fully later on. But this much can be seen at once: *there is more to fear than fear itself.* The sweeps and fluctuations of the inducement to invest are not caused solely by psychological phenomena. The marginal efficiency of capital is not always determined by what the owners of capital *think* they can gain by reinvestment. Eventually there comes a time when, because debt stops expanding, the owners of capital *know for sure* that their capital will not yield a monetary saving.

DEPRESSION ENSUES
WHEN DEBT FAILS TO EXPAND

Let us return to the assumed group of very businesslike enterprises which, out of 10% net profit on $200 billion of sales, are reinvesting $10 billion while adding another $10 billion to their personal savings. And let us assume that the time has come when debt stops expanding. If debt fails to increase it will be impossible for the annual $10 billion monetary savings to materialize. Worse still, *sales* will be reduced by $10 billion. That is, only $190 billion were cash sales; the other $10 billion were credit (debt) sales which will not be made if debt is not expanding. Now, the fact that profits for accumulation fail to materialize is a heavy psychological blow to the inducement to invest. But the fact that sales have fallen off by 5% ($10 billion) makes it painfully clear that additional production facilities are not urgently needed. Why build new plants if all the output of existing plants is not being sold? So, if debt fails to expand, investment will cease—more because of the facts of reduced sales than for less compelling psychological reasons. Further, if the $10 billion of investment is halted, *sales will be reduced by that much more,* for those who were paid this $10 billion in wages, salaries, taxes, etc., to produce new plant and equipment will be cut off without income, and will be unable to buy.

Total sales then, are reduced not only the 5% caused by the failure of debt to expand, but an additional 5% caused by the cessation of investment. This 10% drop in sales calls for a 10% cutback in production. Why produce goods that can't be sold at a profit? Just prior to this cutback the business group's expenditures for wages, salaries, taxes, etc., in producing the goods and services for sale was $180 billion. If production is now cut back 10%, these expenditures by the business group will be reduced to $162 billion (180 — 10% = 162). If the people and their governments are determined to spend no more than their income, they now can buy at the rate of only $162 billion. The 10% cutback in the production rate therefore was not enough; an additional 9% cutback must be made. That is, sales originally were at the rate of $200 billion; we have now reached the point where sales can only be at a rate of $162 billion (200 — 19% = 162).

Reviewing to here, the failure of debt to increase at a rate of $10 billion had led, in a few quick steps, to a $38 billion curtailment of production and income, a cessation of investment, and unemployment of 19% of original manpower and plant capacity. Depression ensues. And the depression becomes deeper and deeper; for the 19% cutback will be found upon further analysis still not to be enough. With each new cutback in production, the people's purchasing power will be reduced, and sales will fall to the new lower level. So production must be cut back some more. Such is the nature of things, then, that *the failure of debt to increase will bring about depression.* Since this is the case, there should be real-life statistics dating from around the time of the crash of 1929 that will illustrate this awkward arrangement.

Table 2-2

Year	Increase in Debt			National Income		Unemployment
1926	$6.3	billion		$77	billion	
1927	8.5	"		76	"	
1928	8.7	"		79	"	
1929	4.3	"		83	"	1,736,000
1930	0.3	"		69	"	4,676,000
1931	−8.8	"	(decrease)	54	"	8,136,000
1932	−6.9	"	"	42	"	11,671,000
1933	−6.0	"	"	39.5	"	13,857,000

You can see in Table 2-2 that 1930 is the year when debt failed to expand (but the *rate* of debt expansion had slackened sufficiently in 1929 to produce incipient depression). The cutback in income (output) and employment in 1930 from the levels of 1929 is quite conspicuous. Further, as shown by the data on income and unemployment, this cutback was not enough. In 1931 there was another cutback. By 1933 the cutback in national income as compared with that of 1929 was about 52%; the cutback in employment about 40%.

These cutbacks measured on an overall national basis do not tell the full story. You see, some American businesses (farming, for example) do not cut back at all. That is, small enterprises do not behave in the manner of our assumed group of businesslike businesses. Some real-life cutbacks occurring in the early years of the great depression which are more in line with the practices of our assumed group of corporations are as follows: pig iron production cut back 80%; private construction cut back 86%; manufacturing plant and equipment expenditures cut back 79%; motor vehicle production cut back 75%, et cetera.

So, it can be seen that the bottom of a great depression can be very low indeed. And the greater proportion of big business there is in the economy the lower it will be.

AGGREGATE DEBT CAN NEVER BE REPAID

The reader now should glance back at Table 2-2 and note in the "Increase in Debt" column that after 1930 the aggregate debt was reduced. That is, there are several annual *decreases* in debt. At first you may be puzzled by the paradox of debt being reduced during the worst years of the depression. What an unusual time for the people to be repaying their debts! How strange that the people should increase their net debt by $21.5 billion in the boom years 1927, 28 and 29, then turn around and *reduce* their debt by $21.7 billion in the depression years of 1931, 32, and 33!

Not strange at all. The boom years were booming because the people were going deeper into debt. The debt was reduced during the depression because the people were being dispossessed and thrown into bankruptcy. You see, when there is prosperity the big owners of capital accumulate fortunes and the general run of people go into debt. When the people refuse to go further into debt, depression ensues. During the depression, the owners of capital lay off employees; and many of these disemployed wage and salaried workers are in debt. Here we have an economic impasse: the owners of capital cut off the incomes of the people who owe them money!

Now, an unemployed debtor soon becomes a delinquent debtor. Under the law, a delinquent debtor may be foreclosed, or bankrupted or dispossessed. After this action is taken, however, the *debt is cancelled.* That is how the debt was reduced during the years 1931-33. *It was not paid off.* Indeed, it is possible to account for most of this $21.7 billion decrease in debt by evaluating data from existing statistics. Table 2-3 gives an accounting of about three-fourths of the decrease.

In considering the data in Table 2-3, note that the "deposits of suspended banks" are analogous to *loans* by suspended banks, and that these banks failed because the loans could not be repaid. If we allow $5,000 unpaid balance (debt) cancelled for each lost farm, and a $3,000 mortgage cancelled for each fore-

Table 2-3

Date	Farms Changing Ownership by Forced Sales, Foreclosures and Related Defaults	Number of Foreclosures (Non-Farm Homes)	Business Failures (Current Liabilities)	Deposit of Suspended Banks
1931	167,000	193,000	$735,310,000	(1930-33)
1932	272,300	248,700	928,313,000	$6,858,633,000
1933	363,500	252,400	502,830,000	

closed home, the debt cancellation represented in Table 3 will add up to $15 billion. Repossessions and uncollected accounts (many "business failures" were small businesses which went under because they could not collect their accounts receivable) would account for most of the remainder.

So, in 1930 the poker game was stopped. It was *not* found practicable to "settle up." In the effort to settle up, however, about 11% of the IOUs were torn up.

The dismal statistics in Table 2-3 may bring back unpleasant memories to those still alive who were dispossessed during that catastrophic depression. At this late date it is impossible to assuage them for their pain, anguish, and wreckage of their dreams. But if there still lingers in the mind of anyone who "lost out" during those bleak years any feeling of guilt, or of failure, it is utterly needless. Those people who "failed" in the early thirties had merely got themselves into debt. But it is the nature of things that aggregate debt *never can be repaid.* These people, as a group, had taken, innocently, a step that could not be retracted, no matter how clever the attempt, or how great the effort. In fact, the first mass effort to repay debt must manifest itself as a cessation of the increase of debt—which will bring on depression. Aggregate debt must be increasing for there to be prosperity. To be employed, the debtors always must be going deeper into debt. If they stop they become unemployed, then delinquent and, finally, dispossessed. Aggregate debt can be reduced by foreclosures and bankruptcies, but it cannot be repaid. There is failure here in our society's institutions, and in our financial conduct. But as for *individual* failure, there is no more here than in growing old or catching cold; it is statistically impossible not to fall victim to such inevitable eventualities.

Let us put this proposition another way. Let us say you went into debt to start a small business, acquire inventory, or buy a farm or home. And let us make one single assumption: within a reasonable time you must either pay off or lose out. Now, do you think that if you are a good businessman or farmer, or worker, you will be able to pay off? And if you do lose out it is because you, personally, are a failure? Not so. If you are trying to pay off a debt when large enough numbers of other people are trying not to go deeper into debt, you will fail. You may be a good businessman, a good farmer, a good workman. But you can't get out of debt unless others are going deeper into debt. What happens to you depends upon what the aggregate of other debtors are doing. No matter how good you are, or how hard you try, if you are in debt when aggregate debt stops expanding, your goose is cooked. Nothing personal about it whatever.

The total (aggregate) net debt includes, besides all individual debts, the sum of all public and corporate debt. Should it happen that either, or both, of these latter two categories are increasing at a rapid rate, then it is possible to repay some private individual debt. During the war years, 1941-44, about $5 billion of individual debts actually was repaid. In those years, you see, the federal government debt increased by $160 billion. It is not likely that corporate debt would increase unless individual or public debt was increasing too. That is, corporations would not incur debt unless other debt was increasing fast enough to buy up the full output of existing corporate facilities. During periods when prosperity is being sustained by the increase in private debt (1922-29 and 1947-76), it is possible for *some* individuals to repay, but only if others are incurring debts at a rate much faster than the lucky ones are paying. Within the complexity of net debt, then, it is possible for there to be some shifting of the burden back and forth among those categories of which it is comprised. But all the while, unless there is depression, the total debt will be increasing. There is no turning back; no relief.

Now, there are some compelling reasons why private debt, especially individual private debt, cannot continually increase over very long periods. Almost every private individual who goes into debt does so with serious intentions of, someday, paying off. So a time surely will come when the individual stops going deeper into debt and makes a try, at least, at repaying. Further, as the individual sinks deeper into debt, the burden of heavy interest charges becomes less tolerable. Indeed, it is mathematically possible for total interest charges to equal, eventually, the total personal income. But it is physically impossible for individuals to go this far. They would starve (by paying out, say, 50% of their income for interest charges before spending for food and clothing) long before this mathematical debt-saturation point was reached. Also, as an individual's debts rise higher and higher, the fear of foreclosure or bankruptcy becomes more worrisome. Then, too, as the debtor becomes obviously insolvent, the creditors become more cautious and refuse to lend him more money.

Private debt, therefore, due to these various compelling reasons, is prevented from expanding greatly for very long. Since this is so, there is small chance for the shifting of debt, within the net debt structure, from public over onto private shoulders. Now, public (government) debt is of such a nature that it cannot be reduced through foreclosure or bankruptcy. So there is little possibility for any significant reduction in public debt. True, upon occasion (1922-29, 1947-51) private debt increases so fast that it is possible for some public debt to be repaid. But, as shown in Table 4, these occasional repayments are not very substantial.

You will note that public debt was reduced by $24.5 billion (while private debt was increasing $139.2 billion) in the postwar years from 1945 to 1951. This, though absolutely large, was relatively small—being something less than 10% of the public debt. Indeed, about $19 billion of this was simply the payback

Table 2-4

Year Ending	Total Outstanding Public Debt	Total Outstanding Private Debt	Total Net Debt Outstanding
1922	$ 30.5 billion	$109.5 billion	140
1929	29.7 "	161.5 "	191
1945	266.5 "	140.7 "	407
1951	242.0 "	279.2 "	521

of excess borrowings of the war loan of 1945. Of course, by 1952, public debt once more was expanding. And by 1955 the reduction had been wiped out: public debt was higher than in 1945!

Public debt, then, being beyond reduction through bankruptcy or foreclosure and practically prevented from being foisted onto private individuals, has about it the quality of permanence. Given the present order, heavy public debt will be with us forever and ever. Worse yet, over the long run, it will grow larger and larger. Ever growing, too, will be the burden of interest that must be paid by the many who are born under this heritage of debt.

DEBT IS OWED BY THE MANY TO THE FEW

Early in November of 1961 the total of our net debt, public and private, passed through the one-trillion-dollar level—and continued to increase. This debt "grew up" in a single lifetime. It reached the $100-billion mark in 1918. It passed the $200-billion level in 1941 and reached $400 billion at the end of World War II. In 1951 it passed $500 billion; 10 years later $1,000 billion. The $1,500-billion level was passed during the summer of 1968 and the two-trillion level late in 1971. By the end of 1973 it had passed $2,500 billion. So, it increased 25-fold in 55 years. On a per capita basis, however, it increased only 13-fold: from $900 per person in 1918 to $12,000 per person in 1973.

It is startling to consider that each baby born in 1973 acquired, along with its layette, an average indebtedness of $12,000. However, much of the publicity given to this enormous debt tends to emphasize mainly the federal portion. Occasional articles in newspapers or magazines may express some alarm at the overall *size* of the debt but express little concern about the *consequences*. Indeed, the opinion-makers seem fairly consistent in their expressed belief that the huge debt poses no danger because (1) we simply owe it to ourselves, or (2) we simply owe it to each other.

Literally, of course, this is true. But it is not actually so simple. Consider the public debt (federal, state and local), which amounts to about $650 billion net in 1975: if this is simply owed to ourselves, are we all rich merely because of the huge public debt? How absurd! Obviously, we cannot all get rich individually by going into debt collectively.

If we consider only private debt (about $2,200 billion in 1975), the fallacy is even more obvious. You see, we can't all get rich by signing IOUs and giving them to each other. Nor can we do it by borrowing at the banks and writing checks to each other. The absurdity here is all the more startling when we realize that this is what we actually do: we borrow money from "others" and pay it out to "others." But our intuition tells us that "we" is one group, and the "others" is another group. Our intuition tells us something else: "we" is a large group; the "others" is a small group.

Scientific studies have turned up evidence to show that this hunch is correct. Surveys of consumer finances conducted by the University of Michigan collect some data[2] on liquid assets held by spending units (families, roughly). These data disclosed that (1) only 1% of spending units held marketable U.S. bonds; (2) only 4% of spending units held liquid assets of $10,000 or more; (3) 56% of all spending units held less than $500 each, and about half of these held none. Another study[3] showed the top 3% of

---

[2]*Federal Reserve Bulletin,* July 1959, pp. 700-723.

[3]Raymond Goldsmith, *A Study of Saving in the United States* (Princeton, 1955).

households (by net worth) owning among them net monetary assets twice as large as the combined net holdings of the bottom 70% of households.

A more rigorous study[4] reported that the top 1% of the population held 30% of the personally held wealth; the top one-tenth of one percent of individuals held over 13%. This study also reports that as the rich get richer, and older, they increase their holdings of cash, bonds, corporate stock, mortgages and notes. For example, this top 1% of the population held nearly 100% of all state and local government bonds held by individuals.

These studies are grouped around the census year 1960, when the total of private and public debt divided by the number of spending units gave an average indebtedness of $16,500 per spending unit. So it would appear that less than 4% of the households had more monetary assets than their average share of the total debt, while more than 96% had less. Near the dividing line that separates net debtors from net creditors are some that about break even. For practical purposes, then, the data support an estimate of 90% of the families in debt; 2% of the families in the money. Further refinement based on a few studies of the very rich would suggest that the top 10% of the top 2% are *really* in the money. For our purposes here we may reasonably conclude that the many owe the few.

SWEAT IS THE STUFF INTEREST IS PAID WITH

By 1974, interest payments on public, mortgage, consumer and other individual debt exceeded $100 billion per year. Since aggregate debt cannot be repaid, the interest charge is theoretically permanent and probably irreducible. Indeed, since aggregate debt tends to get larger over the long run, the total interest charge tends, likewise, to get larger.

According to Keynes, interest is a reward for not hoarding.

---

[4]R. J. Lampman, *The Share of Top Wealth Holders in National Wealth* (Princeton, 1962).

That is, when a man lends money, he is *not* lending money that he intended to spend or invest. Rather, he is lending money that is left over *after* he has spent and invested as much as he wished. In other words, borrowed money is money which, if it had not been lent, *would have been hoarded.* This is really a quite revolutionary idea. Like all such ideas, it is looked upon with some suspicion. Even so, it's a good idea and, so long as it isn't disproved, we may accept it. So, when borrowing money, we must pay a reward (interest) to the lender to dissuade him from hoarding. The amount of reward (rate of interest) we must pay depends, according to Keynes, upon how strongly the lender would like to have hoarded.

These two preceding paragraphs, one of fact and one of theory, lead us directly to a very strange observation: American debtors are paying, annually, over $100 billion interest to a relatively few creditors as a reward to them for *not* having hoarded forty times as much money as there is!

Of course, we understand how the acquisitive refrained from hoarding forty times as much as there is: each time we borrowed money, we used it to pay for that part of the purchase price of all the things sold that represented the profits for accumulation. That is, we borrow money from the owners of capital so we can pay them their price for the goods they've just sold us. Thus, they get the money back to relend to us when we again want to borrow to pay for more goods. It's very simple—just like the IOUs in the poker game; after each hand the cash is back in the pocket of the consistent winner; so the losers must write out a new batch of IOUs to get enough cash to continue the game.

We know, then, how the debt got to be so big (monetary shortfall); we have Keynes's theory to explain why interest must be paid (a reward for not hoarding): and it follows that the intensity of the propensity to hoard sets the basic rate of interest; that is, the rate that would prevail when prices are stable. But there remains one important gap in our understanding of interest: we do not know how we actually make the interest payments.

We could presume, considering all the previous disclosures about debt, that interest is paid with more debt. That is, we go into debt with such ease to acquire goods, we might go deeper into debt (i.e., borrow more money) to pay the interest. However, this presumption turns out to be wrong, at least largely so. And the error is fairly easy to detect. Consider, once more, the group of businesslike enterprises which pays out $190 billion a year and takes in $200 billion. Let us assume that this group has operated profitably at full capacity (that is, there was no attempt on the part of the people to stop going deeper into debt by at least $10 billion a year) for a period, say, of ten years. At the end of this period of prosperity, the total debt would have reached at least $100 billion. And, assuming an interest rate of about 5%, annual interest charges will be at least $5 billion. If, then, in addition to the $10 billion accumulation arising from the business-like operation of the enterprises, the owners wished also to save the interest on their past accumulations, the annual rate of increase of debt would have had to advance from $10 billion to (at least) $15 billion to maintain the same level of consumption, investment, production and employment.

So, the idea of paying interest with borrowed money isn't very practicable. That is, if debt must increase at a rate including interest compounded annually, it would be exceedingly difficult after a relatively few years to keep the system from collapse. Of course, in real life it is becoming more difficult to maintain acceptable levels of employment. But the difficulty is not nearly so great as it would be if the acquisitive actually accumulated at a compound rate. That they do not insist upon this compound rate is readily proved statistically by comparing annual changes in debt with annual interest charges. That is, if the annual interest charge is $10 billion and the acquisitive insisted on adding this to their profit accumulations, the annual increase in debt, in time of prosperity at least, would have to be larger than this, say $15 or $20 billion. You see, there must be some debt left over to provide a profit for accumulation from the regular operation of business enterprise. The data compiled in Table 2-5 show this not

Table 2-5

(1)	(2)	(3)	(4)	(5)	(6)
			Annual Interest		Relative Unemployment (Full
Year Ending	Total Net Debt (ΣD)	Change in Debt (D)	Charge (r)×(ΣD)	D−(r)ΣD	Employment =0%)
1920	135.4	7.4	6.8	+ 0.6	9%
1921	135.8	0.4	6.9	− 6.5	27
1922	140.0	4.2	7.2	− 3.0	22
1923	146.4	6.4	7.6	− 1.2	10
1924	153.1	6.7	8.0	− 1.3	13
1925	162.7	9.6	8.3	+ 1.6	11
1926	169.0	6.3	8.7	− 2.4	9
1927	177.5	8.5	9.1	− 0.6	8
1928	186.2	7.7	9.7	− 2.0	7
1929	191.1	4.9	9.9	− 5.0	5
1930	191.4	0.3	9.9	− 9.6	15
1931	182.6	− 8.8	9.3	−18.1	26
1932	175.7	− 7.9	8.6	−16.5	38
1933	169.7	− 6.0	8.0	−14.0	39
1934	172.6	2.9	8.0	− 5.1	34
1935	175.9	3.3	8.2	− 4.9	32
1936	181.4	5.5	8.3	− 2.8	27
1937	183.3	1.9	8.4	− 6.5	23
1938	180.9	− 2.4	8.3	−10.7	30
1939	184.5	3.6	8.4	− 4.8	27
1940	190.9	6.4	8.6	− 2.2	24
1941	212.6	20.7	9.4	+11.3	17
1942	260.6	48.0	9.9	+38.1	8
1943	314.3	53.7	11.0	+42.7	3
1944	371.6	57.3	12.2	+45.1	2
1945	407.2	36.6	13.1	+23.5	3
1946	398.7	− 8.5	13.5	−22.0	7
1947	416.5	16.4	14.6	+ 1.8	6
1948	430.8	14.3	15.8	− 1.5	6
1949	446.7	15.9	16.5	− 3.4	10
1950	485.8	35.1	18.3	+16.8	10
1951	521.2	35.4	19.8	+15.6	8
1952	556.1	34.9	21.0	+14.9	7
1953	583.5	29.4	22.0	+ 7.4	6
1954	605.5	20.0	23.1	− 3.1	10

Explanation of Table 2-5: Columns 2, 3, 4 and 5 are in billions of dollars. Column 6 is my evaluation of unemployment *including underemployment*; i.e., even if everybody was employed, if they were working only half the usual weekly working hours, the relative unemployment would be 50%. (Less than 10% unemployment would be considered "boom" times.) Column 3 is the increase in debt for the year. Column 4 is the annual interest charge estimated rather conservatively. Column 5 is the annual change in debt *minus* the annual interest charge; if this difference is negative during boom times it proves quite conclusively that the interest charge is not being accumulated to any very great extent. The negative values for 1926-29, 1948-49, and 1954 practically clinch the case.

to be the case. Especially conclusive is the fact that during certain prosperous years—1926-29, 1948-49, and 1954—the new debt is actually *less* than the total interest charge. Table 2-5, by the way, is merely offered as evidence; it need not be studied at length.

It is quite certain, then, that the rich do not actually accumulate the interest on our debts. Further, it would be surprising if these interest receipts were reinvested by the rich. You see, investment is the first step in acquiring the fortune upon which interest is collected. That is, the fruit of investment is monetary savings (the melon that is cut); the fruit of monetary savings is interest (something that derives from the melon without diminishing it). We must conclude, therefore, that the rich *spend*, i.e., consume, their interest receipts. Investment is the goose that lays the golden eggs (monetary savings), and these golden eggs are capable of producing other little eggs at a rate equal to the rate of interest. It is this endless supply of little eggs that is eaten.

In testing this conclusion against the facts, let us start by dividing the acquisitive into two groups called (after Keynes) *entrepreneurs* and *rentiers*. The *entrepreneurs* are those seeking to increase or accumulate fortunes by businesslike operation (and succeeding insofar as debt is expanding). The *rentiers* are those who have long since cut their melons and receive income chiefly in the form of interest. If the *rentiers* (i.e., the idle rich) are content to live off the interest of our debts (and do not seek to increase the principal amount of their holdings), then all of the annual increase in debt will be available to the *entrepreneurs* to reward them in their struggle for personal fortunes. Prosperity and high employment, then, can be maintained by a relatively constant rate of increase in debt. The rate would tend to rise only as capital and industry become more monopolized. So, it would not be necessary for the annual increase in debt to exceed annual interest payments. This explanation fits the factual data shown in Table 2-5.

Furthermore, our conclusion explains, perhaps, why the present order has escaped complete collapse down to this late date. You see, as our debts increase, if the rich spend all their interest income, their propensity to consume is increased. And this increase in consumption will have a beneficial effect upon employment, especially during depressions. That is, as more and richer *rentiers* are created, more employment is required to provide them with the larger quantities of goods and services they consume. During a depression, this additional employment will loom larger percentagewise, providing some cushion.

But we have a theory far from favorable to the existing order. For, if we are on the right track, it is possible now to say how we make the interest payments; we make the payments with goods and services—that is, with the fruits of our labor. The general run of people contract an aggregate debt that never can be repaid and on which the interest charges will continue indefinitely. And we pay these interest charges by working to produce the large quantities of goods and services consumed by the rich. The fortunes of the rich are born of debt; the interest on this debt is paid with the perpetual labor of the people who owe. Much debt, indeed, is contracted by the general run of productive workers who consume goods faster than their income permits. But, for the temporary joy of spending this artificial purchasing power, must be paid the terrible price of permanent bondage.

While, therefore, it is the nature of debt that an increasing amount of it will promote prosperity, encourage investment, and make the rich richer; and that the absence of an increasing amount of it will bring about depression, discourage investment, and cause the debtors to be dispossessed; and that, in the aggregate, it never can be repaid, debt also bears interest. It is the nature of interest that it must be paid forever to the creditors out of the fruits of the labor of the debtors. So, by going into debt, free men deliver themselves into economic bondage.

3

THE FARM PROBLEM

> The dangers that menace our civilization do not come
> from the weakness of the springs of production. What it
> suffers from, and what, if a remedy be not applied, it
> must die from is unequal distribution.
>
> HENRY GEORGE
> *Progress and Poverty*

From long in the past, farmers have been plagued with
problems. There were problems enough just in the raising of
delicate plants and stubborn animals. But the plants and animals
were subject to attack by, among other things, insects, disease,
and the weather. So the basic problems were compounded.
Modern technology made life easier for the plants and animals,
but it complicated life for the farmer. Complex machines, toxic
chemicals, electrical gadgets, special seeds and fertilizers, etc.,
are forced upon his attention in a never-ending stream. So the
farmer's problems range from the ancient ones of agriculture and
husbandry to the modern ones of agronomy, chemistry, bacteri-
ology and mechanical engineering. And yet, when we now speak
of the "farm problem," we mean something to do with *economics*.

The "farm problem" is that of the farmer being squeezed between falling prices for the things he sells, and rising prices for
those he buys. More precisely it is the squeeze between costs
rising faster than revenue, or not falling so fast. This squeeze is
often called the "scissors problem." This name aptly describes
what happens to the farmer: he is caught between the closing
blades of an economic scissors.

PARITY—AND THE PERIOD 1910-21

The first really harsh squeeze of the scissors came in the early 1920s. The farmers then looked back with longing to the period 1910-14, a happier time when farm prices were considered to be on a "par" with industrial prices. Those were the so-called "parity years," and the prices that prevailed then are still used as the base for computing the "parity ratio." This ratio, which measures the farmers' relative economic standing, is determined by dividing the index of the prices the farmer receives by the index of prices he pays. So, for the base period, 1910-14, the formula was: 100 divided by 100 = 100%. And 100% of parity is "par."

By 1917, the impact of World War I had pushed these price indexes upward from 100 each to 175 received and 148 paid. This gave the farmer 118% of his parity share (i.e., 175 divided by 148 = 118%). This 18% bonus for the farmers prevailed, on the average, through 1917 and 1918, and provided a strong incentive for increasing farm production.

It is so logical that farmers would try to increase their output in response to a high parity ratio that it seems needless to argue the point. But it is necessary to point out that, so far as each individual farmer is concerned, it is *not easy* to increase production. You see, during times of *normal* prices the farmer tries to operate at full capacity. So, when prices for his products rise, there isn't much slack he can take up to substantially increase his output. Besides, there is a fixed area within the boundaries of a farm, and a limit to the hours in a farmer's workday. So, he can't increase output quickly, as industry does, simply by putting on extra shifts or setting up new banks of machines. Actually the average farmer's best chance to increase output is through increased *productivity:* more fertilizer, better land use, soil conservation, improved seeds, more mechanization, less waste, etc. Increasing farm output by these methods was always a slow and difficult process. Even so, farmers generally did succeed in increasing output (and largely by higher productivity), when spurred by a rising parity ratio.

The favorable parity ratio of 1917-18, however, didn't last very long. In 1919, the ratio fell to 109%; to 104% in 1920; and to an average of 75% for the depression year of 1921. Thus the blades of the scissors were closed. In only four years the farmers' economic standing fell from 18% above par to 25% below par.

THE DEPRESSION SQUEEZE

In time of depression, industrial production and employment are reduced. The 1921 depression brought a 24% cutback in industrial output, and unemployment rose to about 24% of the labor force. Each of these typical depression events has a quick effect on the farmer. First, the cutback of industrial output reduces the supply of such products. This causes their prices to rise relative to the prices for farm products. Second, the cutback in employment lowers the effective demand for farm products (as the incomes of workers fall and they must reduce spending). This reduces the price received by farmers. Thus both blades of the scissors are squeezed.

There are many industrial products that the farmer *must* buy: machinery parts, fertilizer, chemicals, gas and oil, hardware, etc. During depressions their supply is reduced by the cutback of industrial production. So, their prices are held up. But this does not make them less necessary to the farmer. He must buy.

On the other hand, the farmer must sell his products. Most are perishable or too bulky to store. So they must be marketed even if there is less money to buy them because many consumers are unemployed. In the free agricultural markets (prior to the time of the New Deal) the prices of farm products were determined by the amount of them sent to market to sell, and the amount of money brought to the marketplace to buy them. A sudden reduction in the amount of this purchasing power (and a consequent fall in the price of farm products) did not relieve the farmer of his need to send his products to market. He simply had to sell!

From 1920 to 1921 the prices *received* by farmers fell 41%. But the prices *paid* by farmers fell only 18%—a greater fall being prevented by the 24% cutback in industrial output.

MORE FARM PRODUCTION FOR LESS PAY

Previously it was noted that farmers try to increase production when farm prices (or the parity ratio) are rising. Now, it so happens that the average farmer reacts the same way to *falling* prices. That is, when faced with a falling income due to lower farm prices, or a lower parity ratio, the typical farmer—especially if he owns his farm and equipment—is stimulated to *increase* production. He does this in the attempt to maintain his income.

We are inclined to think that the prime force in our economy is the profit incentive. But there are really *two* sides to this: the desire for gain, and the fear of loss. Actually, if we look at the past objectively, we will see that the fear of loss seems the stronger of the two. The more violent strikes take place when labor is threatened with a *cut* in wages (e.g., the coal strike of 1919, and the British general strike in 1926) rather than when labor is seeking a raise. Stock market prices usually fall faster than they had risen—as operators seek to forestall losses. In recessions the big corporations cut back their operations to reduce costs faster than they had expanded output when their prices had been rising.

As for the farmer, a large part of his costs is fixed. His income depends almost solely on selling his products at unit prices over which he has no control. So, it is perfectly normal for him to react to the fear of loss by *increasing* production. Raising less will not restore a falling income. On the contrary, he must sell *more*, at the going market price, even though that price is low.

This tendency for the farmer to increase output in the face of unfavorable prices attracts no sympathy from the businessman. They and the industrialists consider it to be wrongheadedness. After all, it is opposite from the way *they* do it. To businessmen, it simply doesn't seem businesslike. Since these businessmen are often in high places in public life, the fallacy that the farm problem is caused by "overproduction" is given too much publicity. In the opinion of businessmen, increasing output in the face of falling prices is not the right thing for anyone to do. And they leap to the conclusion that high production is the *cause* of low farm prices. Actually, of course, it is often the other way around. That is, low farm prices cause high farm production.

We noted above that the fear of loss seems to be a stronger motivation than the desire for gain. In fact, there is evidence to indicate that farmers work harder to increase output when their incomes are falling than when they are rising. It is true, of course, that this extra production does have a further depressing effect on farm prices. Indeed, if it weren't that this extra production came with such difficulty—at the most a few percentage points a year—we should have to count this proclivity to produce as one of the underlying causes of the farm problem. Actually, however, it was seldom more than a minor factor.

It is worth noting at this point that another theory—that a "collapse" of foreign markets after World War I was the, or a, cause of the farm problem—is not borne out by the facts. In a study of this phase of the farm problem, Mr. Louis Bean of the U.S. Department of Agriculture discovered (see *The Changing Composition of Gross Farm Income Since the Civil War*) that 17.6% of gross farm income derived from foreign markets during the period 1914-18. For the postwar period, 1919-23 (when these markets are thought to have "collapsed"), the figure actually rose a bit to 17.8%.

THE BIG BOOM—1922 TO 1929

We have seen that in 1921 the scissors problem was harshly driven home to the farmers. And that the sharp squeeze of 1921 was caused almost solely by the sharp depression of that year. After 1921, the American economy recovered rapidly, and proceeded into the "roaring twenties." But there were no "roaring" twenties for the farmers. True, there was some recovery from the low parity ratio of 1921. But the ratio did not get back to par during the entire boom. In the five-year period that ended in 1921, the farmers enjoyed the moderate prosperity of a parity ratio that averaged 105%. But in the next five-year period, 1922-26, the parity ratio averaged only 86%. There was no Big Boom for the farmers.

Incidentally, the Department of Agriculture made a comparative study of these two five-year periods. The results were reported in the 1927 *Yearbook of Agriculture*. They showed that the output of crops was 5% greater, and the output of animal products 15% greater, in the latter five-year period than in the former. Here is factual proof that farmers increased their production in the face of falling prices. But the study disclosed, too, that this increase was not enough to be called "overproduction." In the face of a 19-point drop in the average parity ratio between the two periods, the farmers succeeded in increasing crop production only an average of 1% a year. Animal products increased only 3% a year. Since, during these two five-year periods, the population of the country was growing at the average rate of 1.6% a year, it is clear that there was no real "overproduction."

Even so, the scissors problem continued—becoming almost chronic. In the top years of the boom—1927, 1928, and 1929—the parity ratio averaged only 88%. This was better than the 75% ratio of 1921. But it was quite low enough to indicate scissors pressure even in the absence of depression. So, obviously the depression squeeze is not the *only* cause of the scissors problem. It appears that at least two other forces are involved: a price-category squeeze, and a debt squeeze.

THE PRICE-CATEGORY SQUEEZE

It has been known for hundreds of years that all prices are not determined in the same way. Even Adam Smith, in 1776, recognized competitive price as the "lowest which can be taken"; monopoly price the "highest which can be got." Competitive price prevails when there are many sellers and many buyers; monopoly price, when there is only one seller for many buyers.

Now, absolute monopolies, i.e., *one* seller, are not very important in our economy. Rather, the industrial part of our economy consists mainly of "monopolistic competition": a *few* sellers for many buyers. Studies of this arrangement make it clear that prices under these monopolistic conditions are higher, in relation to costs, than competitive prices. To state the matter in jargon: when there are many sellers for many buyers, the price tends to *equal* marginal cost (the cost of the last item produced); but when there are only a *few* sellers for many buyers the price tends to *exceed* marginal cost. Worse yet, in this latter case, the marginal cost itself often includes advertising and other special selling costs.

To restate it simply: the prices paid by farmers are categorically higher than the prices they receive. This creates a scissors problem independent of depression: a squeeze between two categories of prices. This squeeze gets worse as industry becomes more monopolized (that is, as ownership becomes more concentrated). The trend toward monopoly had advanced so far by the late 1920s that a well-defined scissors problem existed even though industrial employment and output were high. In fact, by 1929, at the very top of the boom, the American farmers were in such obvious financial distress that the Hoover Administration created the Federal Farm Board with a half-billion-dollar fund to try to do something about the situation.

THE DEBT SQUEEZE

The 1920 decade saw the coming-of-age of monopolistic industry. But, it was also a period of rapid growth of consumer and mortgage debt. In those ten years, mortgage debt more than doubled. Consumer debt grew by leaps and bounds. By the end of 1929, individual and non-corporate debt reached a total of 73 billion dollars. This was about equal to a year's national income. To make matters worse, so far as the scissors problem was concerned, the farmers themselves owed over $13 billion. Farm income in those days was about $6 billion a year. So, farm debt was more than twice annual farm income. Just as you would expect, these heavy debts also pressed on both blades of the scissors!

All debtors, of course, are consumers. By 1929, individual consumers were in debt, on the average, by more than a year's income. So, their buying power (used in part to buy farm products) was reduced over 6% just because of their interest payments. More important, such debts require heavy payments on the principal, too. So the money available to take to market for food is much reduced, even when there is no actual loss of income from unemployment. (Observe, too, that the payments of interest and principal are made to people who will *not* use it to buy food. Such people had more than enough money for that purpose, else they would not have had excess funds to lend out in the first place.)

As for the average farmer, his available net income was reduced more than 12%, for *he* owed more than two years' income. Besides, had he gone into debt to buy farm machinery (produced by a few sellers who sell to many farmers), he would have paid monopolistic price (by way of payments of principal) *plus* interest.

Reviewing to this point: we see that, in time of depression, prices *paid* by farmers are held up relatively by the cutback of industrial production; prices *received* by farmers are forced down absolutely by the lack of purchasing power of the unemployed. In an economy with much monopolistic enterprise, prices *paid* by farmers, even under full-employment conditions, are raised into a distinctly higher category than the prices they receive. In an economy heavy with debt the farmer's income is cut because of the interest and principal payments that consumers must withdraw from their current income before they go to market for food. And the farmer's costs are increased by the interest on *his* debts.

Now, let us examine the havoc created by all three squeezes acting together.

THE BIG SQUEEZE: 1930-32

In 1929, the year the boom ended, the farmers' parity ratio averaged only 89%. This was 11 points below par. In 1930, it dropped 9 points to 80%. In 1931 it averaged 65%. The average from 1932 was 55%: 45 points below par. The full horror of this 55% parity ratio can be seen by recognizing that the farmer's price position was only 55% as favorable as was industry's, and industry was in the trough of its worst depression. Putting it another way, consider this: imagine that you and a group of your fellowmen were working for a large company and all were receiving $100 per week; suddenly the salaries of all the others were cut to $70, but *yours was cut to $38.50*. Then you would experience how it felt to be a farmer in 1932.

For those interested in the grim statistics, the following are furnished. From 1929 to 1932 industrial production was cut back 47%. Unemployment increased by 10,000,000. The average price for the farmers' grain, in that short span of three years, fell 60%. The price of farm machinery and equipment, however, fell only 14%. In 1929 the interest burden on the $191 billion total net debt amounted to about 12% of that year's national income. By 1932 this interest burden had risen to about 20% because the national income had sagged almost 50% to $42 billion. As for the farmers, their net income (after the payment of interest charges) *dropped 70%*.

There are also some statistics that should startle those who believe the "overproduction" theory: from 1929 to 1932 the index of farm production increased only 1%. However, this small increase was not the result of the farmers not trying. You see, the Hoover Farm Board believed the "overproduction" theory too. In 1931, when farm production was up 5% over 1929, the Board urged the farmers to *reduce their crop acreage for 1932 by 30%*. It is interesting to note that this was the first federal effort toward a governmental "policy of scarcity," and it was a whopper: it was a move to reduce the food supply by almost one-third. Luckily for the people, the farmers followed their own economic instincts: ignoring the Farm Board, they planted an acreage in 1932 *exceeding* that of 1931. A policy of scarcity is against the farmers' principles. Largely due to the drought, however, the increased acreage did not actually produce an increase in crops. Then too, in 1932, over 4% of all farms changed hands through forced sales and related defaults. Actually, this was about 275,000 farms. With this many farms being foreclosed in a single year, certainly there was some loss of farm production. It's difficult to get in the crops when the sheriff is on your back. But no one recorded how much was lost. In any event, it wasn't the farmers' fault; they would have preferred to stay on their farms and bring in the harvest.

We have now briefly covered the history of the farm problem from 1910 through 1932. And we have examined the main economic causes underlying the problem. But there are other aspects of economics so closely related to the farm problem that they should not be omitted. These are discussed briefly below.

THE SPECTER OF DIMINISHING RETURNS

In emphasizing that farmers increase their output whether prices are rising or falling, it was not mentioned that some other people deserve part of the credit. True, the farmer deserves credit for the final effort. But it is really the men of science who make it possible for the farmer to succeed: chemists, agronomists, botanists, researchers in many fields and, of course, the engineers who design farm machinery.

As a team, scientists, engineers and the farmer have been so successful, so far, that one hesitates to suggest there is anything they cannot do. However, in theory, there is, eventually, a point of diminishing returns: a point beyond which greater effort only brings *less* production. Sometime in the future there will be this other, more deadly, scissors problem—when the press of excessive population pushes the fixed acreage of arable land beyond its point of maximum productivity and into the vortex of diminishing returns. This theoretical problem of the future has little to do with the American economy, just yet. But the fact that American farmers have consistently increased their productivity under all economic conditions has been strongly emphasized. So, it seems important to point out that there is a theoretical limit to the process. Professor Taussig, the great Harvard economist of a generation ago, described the problem as follows:

> For the community as a whole the tendency to diminishing returns on each several plot of land must be accepted as an obstacle to the indefinite advance of production and population and as a limit which must be soberly faced in all schemes of social reconstruction. (*Principles of Economics,* vol. II, p. 70)

COMPETITIVE OPERATION

America, we must note, is a nation with increasing population. So, it is absolutely vital for there to be increasing farm productivity. It is not surprising, then, that farm productivity has received much attention from economists. Professor Ralph Blodgett, University of Illinois economist, explains this process as follows:

> In the absence of monopolistic tendencies, the farmer is unable to pursue profits by restricting rather than expanding out-put or by maintaining rigid prices thru periods of good and bad business. . . . he is likely to continue to operate at or near full capacity even when market conditions are unfavorable. (*Comparative Economic Systems*, p. 231)

At this point, without further argument, we can take a stand on the question of competitive operation versus monopolistic operation for agriculture. Previously we noted the difference between competitive price and monopolistic price. Now we note the vital difference in the production practices of the two types of enterprise: it is the difference between steadily rising production and fluctuating production. Perhaps we can live without steady production of many industrial products. But it is certainly obvious that we *must* have steady production of agricultural products. Widely fluctuating farm production, you see, would mean feast *and famine*.

So, it seems clear, beyond reasonable doubt, that American democracy should cast its lot on the side of competitive operation in American farming. And all those benefits, such as centralized management, mass production (but not always *full* production), large scale marketing, research and engineering that are commonly claimed for big-business enterprise would be as dust in the balance.

ABSENTEE OWNERSHIP

Perhaps you have noted that farm tenants and sharecroppers have been excluded from the main argument. They, too, suffer when the scissors are closed. And they do form a significant part of American agriculture. They were excluded because they are not so dependable as owner-operators. You see, there are not such compelling reasons for tenants and croppers to respond to the pressure of economic forces in the same laudable manner as do farm owner-operators. This difference between tenants and croppers on the one hand, and owner-operators on the other, is considered very important by economists. For instance, Professor Taussig wrote:

> No stimulus to the best use of land is comparable to that which comes from secure possession, from the certainty that he who makes it yield abundantly will reap the results of his industry. And no kind of secure possession is so effective to this end as untrammeled ownership. (*Principles of Economics,* vol. II, p. 81)

Actually, full ownership of a farm has favorable aspects beyond the purely economic ones. The individual pride of ownership and the dignity deriving from the social worth of his occupation are priceless things. These make the owner-operator a sound citizen concerned with the problems of his community and its social capital such as schools, churches and roads. And the love for the land is not so different from the love for a child: none is so great as that which you feel for your own. Further, a surprising new theory, germane to farm ownership, appeared in 1966. In Robert Ardrey's *The Territorial Imperative* evidence was presented suggesting that ownership of territory actually endows the proprietor with enhanced energy and resolve.

Tenant farming is not so. There is less reason for pride, less dignity, less citizenship. Their absence shows in areas of the country where tenant farming predominates. People move frequently. Roads, schools and churches are rundown. The land may show signs of mistreatment. Generally the land is not farmed; it is "mined." Soil conservation is only a vague abstraction to the average tenant farmer. He must get from the land what he can during his term. Future productivity is not his business.

Actually, it goes deeper than this. The landlord often urges the tenant to exploit the land. According to a report by U.S. Department of Agriculture, "From the standpoint of soil conservation, the development of farm tenancy and absentee ownership is of significance primarily through its effects on land use practices. In the case of tenancy at least two parties are looking to the land as a source of income. If all parties who have to depend for their income on agriculture had the right attitude towards the land, that is a long-time interest in the maintenance of the producing power of the land, tenancy would not be associated with eroding soil and neglected structures. As it is, however, tenancy too often causes the tenant and sometimes the landowner to be interested only in the highest possible immediate income from the land regardless of its future productivity." We can see in this a warning of the scissors problem of the future: diminishing returns.

There can be little question, then, that farm tenancy and sharecropping are not only less desirable than owner-operation, but clearly *undesirable*. It was due to the flaws in the economy that farm tenancy and sharecropping increased steadily from 1880 until 1935. The "scissors problem" and the foreclosure of farm mortgages—both of them built-in aspects of the American economy—were in large part to blame for this deplorable tide of events. By 1935, of the total of 6,800,000 American farms, only 3,900,000 (or 57%) were occupied by the owners, and 40% of them were encumbered by mortgages.

Happily, this trend was reversed during the years when liberal administrations were in political power. By 1945, 67% of American farms were occupied by the owners, and farm debt had been reduced to about 10% of the total value of American farm property. Unfortunately, the policies of the liberals did not solve the problem of farmland ownership; they only eased it temporarily. As we shall see in the next chapter, there is more trouble ahead.

This brief review of farm tenancy and sharecropping shows beyond doubt that absentee ownership of farmland is unsatisfactory. In light of the main argument, however, this negative statement hides the really important point. It is the positive conclusion, rather, that discloses the underlying principle. This is now stated in the words of Professor Taussig:

A wide diffusion of the ownership of land and a predominance of cultivation by the owners are the most wholesome agricultural conditions. (Principles of Economics, p. 80)

We now resume the narrative:

THE NEW DEAL: 1933-52

Not for one minute since May 1933 have the farmers been subjected to the full, unmitigated force of the "scissors." It is true that many disturbing things were done after that date. Cotton was plowed under. Little pigs were slaughtered. Grain was stored in abandoned schoolhouses and the holds of old ships. Potatoes were dyed blue and buried. Butter was stored to become rancid, etc. There can be little doubt that the New Deal did many things—and a lot of them were wrong. But never again was the *full* effect of the "scissors" allowed to be applied to the farmers. After May 1933, therefore, a study of the farm problem inevitably becomes a study of New Deal efforts to thwart it. A lifetime would be required to evaluate all the New Deal treatments of the farm problem. In this chapter the whole era can be given only brief review and comments.

Without doubt the many efforts of the New Deal actually led to many fine results. The trend toward increased farm tenancy was halted, and later reversed. Forced sales and foreclosures were steadily reduced until, in 1946, they reached the low rate of 1910-14. Farm debt was reduced. Farm co-ops were encouraged. Soil conservation on a national scale was started. Much submarginal land, already beyond its point of diminishing returns, was retired from cultivation and returned to nearer its natural state, providing improved conditions for our vanishing wildlife and for the long pull back to useful fertility. Further, the farmers' real income was increased.

But the New Deal *did not achieve a long-range solution of the farm problem.* The main effort of the New Deal was a deliberately planned restriction of farm production. So, the last great stronghold of competitive enterprise in America was infused, by fiat, with some of the evils of monopolistic enterprise. Later, some New Deal economists labeled this method "merely a balance of abuses" and admitted that it was only a "temporary means."

Now, no reasonable person would have accused the New Deal of trying to starve the people. Roosevelt himself said that the legislative aims were toward "adequacy of supply but not glut" and "insurance before the fact instead of government subsidy after the fact." "It is shameless misrepresentation," he said, "to call this a policy of scarcity." It is to be noted, however, that the "plow-under" system was largely replaced by the "ever-normal granary" concept of crop storage as early as 1938. This was an improvement.

And, by 1940, the error of scarcity economics was admitted. In October of that year the New Deal Department of Agriculture submitted to the Temporary National Economic Committee of Congress an economic report: *Agriculture and the National Economy.* This was monograph 23 of a series on concentration of economic power. The closing paragraphs of this report are quoted below:

Most of the government programs for farm aid such as parity payments, crop loans, surplus purchases, and the like can only be defended as temporary means of relieving farm distress which has been occasioned by imperfections in our economic system which have been discussed. Extensions of special privileges to the farmer is not a remedy for the exist-

ence of special privilege elsewhere in the system, but merely
a balance of abuses.

In the long run the farm problem will have to be solved
not on the farm alone but in the general industrial and economic system whose defects have created the problem. Full
output and employment in industry would increase the demand for farm products, would draw off the surplus farm
population and would lower the prices farmers pay. (*Agriculture and the National Economy,* U.S. Government Printing
Office, 1940, p. 42)

The important thing about monograph 23 was that, for all
practical purposes, the truth was out: the farm problem is a
symptom of deep-seated disease within the body economic. And
the treatment of symptoms cannot be expected to cure the
disease. The unemployment and the reduction in industrial output during depressions, together with monopolistic price, and
farm and consumer indebtedness—these were the major causes
of the farm problem. Since none of these causes had been
eliminated it is easy to understand why "parity payments, crop
loans, surplus purchases, and the like" were still with us when
the New Deal left office at the end of 1952.

CHANGE FOR THE WORSE: 1953-68

Not only were the "temporary means" still with us when the
New Deal lost the election of 1952, but the farm problem was
with us too. In 1952, crop-support loans increased to nearly
double the year-end total of 1951; farm debt increased 10% and
the parity ratio fell 7 points. At that point the Republicans took
office.

With the change of administration, things got worse. During
the first four years of the Eisenhower regime more subsidy
money was spent on agriculture than in the preceding twenty
years. By 1956 the stored surpluses were three times as large as
they had been in 1952. During Eisenhower's second term the
farm problem continued to get worse. The strangely "business-

like" idea that farm products should be made scarcer, first put into effect by the New Deal in 1933 when part of the cotton crop actually was plowed under, continued as the dominant idea. And in 1957, a corporate-owned farm in Arizona was paid $209,710.80 for not growing cotton in the first place. To many, this seemed just as nutty in 1957 as plowing under had seemed in 1933.

At this point we interrupt the time flow of the narrative to take stock. It is 1958 and many farmers were using a new fertilizer, anhydrous ammonia, which could increase crop yields by 50% in a single year if generously applied. Obviously rapid changes were occurring down on the farm. Might not this indicate that changes had taken place in the farm problem itself?

Indeed they had. Fertilizer, of course, was part of it. Between 1950 and 1960 the production of both phosphoric acid (a concentrated fertilizer ingredient) and synthetic anhydrous ammonia had more than tripled. In the same period the yield per acre of both wheat and sorghum had more than doubled. Just between 1954 and 1958 the national increase in the production per acre for corn increased by 25%. So, the old days when productivity could increase by only a few points a year had been superseded.

Another important change was in machinery and equipment. For quite some time the use of farm machinery had been increasing; and so had the efficiency of the machinery itself. The main effect of this was an increase in farm labor productivity. From 1950 to 1960 the value of machinery and equipment on farms increased by 84%. In the same period farm output per man hour increased by 90%. This latter, like the output per acre, showed that the old rate of increase of only a few points per year had been greatly surpassed.

As with all change, there were, in all this, mixed blessings. The farmers, with scientific and engineering help, proved by their bountiful production that diminishing returns were no danger yet. But they also proved that they now could *overproduce* in the sense that supply could be increased rapidly enough to seriously depress prices. True, they had, as yet, overproduced only under the stimulus of federal acreage restrictions and price supports. But the possibility of this new squeeze—overproduction —adding to the other causes of the farm problem was now established.

The astounding increase in farm labor productivity had several facets. First it established that fewer people were needed on the farms to provide the food for more people in the nation as a whole. In the 1950 decade, over 7 million people were released from the farm economy. This was a 32% reduction in farm population and it occurred during a 10-year period when real farm income was declining by 30%. So, it had the effect of forestalling the social unrest that a 30% loss in real income might otherwise have caused. That is, a 30% smaller pie caused no farm revolt since there were 32% fewer farm people to divide it. The social unrest was shifted elsewhere. Some of those released from farm work did, perhaps, become doctors, skilled workers and business executives. But many millions, with more hopes than skills, moved into the cities, largely because they had nowhere else to go. Here they crowded into the slums. Later, their hopes and patience exhausted, they exploded into the riots of the 1960 decade.

In all this rapid change little notice was taken of one worsening aspect of the farm problem. With the farmers increasing their purchases of machinery and chemicals they were biasing the price-category squeeze against themselves. Simply by increasing the proportion of monopolistic-price items they bought they were pressing the parity ratio downward to their own disadvantage.

In time—said Veblen—immutable rules of conduct enforced under progressively changing conditions should logically result in a muddle. And so they did. The eight Eisenhower years of struggle with the farm problem produced the following results: (1) The cost of stored surpluses increased from $2½ billion to $9¼ billion; (2) the annual monetary loss on handling these surpluses increased from about $70 million in 1952 to $800 million in 1960; (3) despite a 20% increase in farm output, farm income fell 20%— actually, real farm income (corrected for inflation) fell nearly

30%; (4) farm debt increased more than 70%, and by 1960 the farmers were back to their 1929 status of being in debt more than two full years of farm income; (5) the parity ratio fell from 100 to 80, the result of a 16% drop in farm prices and a 4% increase in prices paid by farmers.

Then, in 1961, the Democrats resumed power, and the farm problem got worse! Farm subsidy payments soon increased to above $1 billion per year and by 1966 exceeded $3 billion. In this latter year one California farm received $2,397,000 for not growing cotton. A single corporate farm collected over $7 million in subsidy payments during the last two years of the Democratic administration. Even so, in 1968 the parity ratio averaged 6 points lower than 1961, and farm debt had risen to nearly 3½ times the 1968 net farm income.

So it is obvious that the farm problem had grown worse, not better, after 35 years of federal effort to correct it. At the end of this chapter is a table showing the economic decline from 1945 to 1970. This span of years neatly embraces "the good years," 1948-67, the 20 years called by Galbraith the "most benign era in the history of the industrial economy—without panic, crises, depression." In this realitively stable setting we can see the underlying cause of the farm problem in its basic simplicity: *the farm problem is mainly the toll of monopolization.* In an economy that is part monopolistic (industry) and part competitive (farming) the *gains* of the monopolists are balanced by a relative *loss* in the competitive sector. Since the concentration in industry shows no signs of abating, or being stopped, it is quite certain that this basic aspect of the farm problem will persist, so that yet another Democratic administration will find it waiting for them when they next take office.

In 1969 the Nixon administration took office and by 1970 a sharp recession was underway. Real farm income fell and farm debt increased. In 1971 the parity ratio averaged out at 70—the lowest year since 1934. Looking ahead to the 1972 election, the Nixon administration, by greatly increasing subsidy payments, arranged for the set-aside of 56 million acres of crop land: 20 million acres of wheat and 36 million acres of feed grains were to be out of production for 1972. So, farm income increased, the parity ratio rose to 74 and the farmers voted for Richard Nixon. But there was a price to pay: American food production was reduced by 2%.

By a fateful coincidence, this drop in food output meshed with crop failures in Russia and India. Quite suddenly the world was short of food, and American farm prices skyrocketed. The parity ratio, which had fallen to 68 in September 1971, rose to 102 by August 1973. It fell back again to 68 by March 1975. But history had made its point: world population now was pressing so hard against the world's agricultural capacity that a sizable disruption in food output anywhere on the globe meant crisis and famine, somewhere.

For the rest of the world—pending the eventual Malthusian crunch and the accompanying onset of diminishing returns—the worst danger is that of crop failure in America. But for us there is a more pressing threat which may materialize without much warning and in the not too distant future. The next chapter is concerned with this potential danger, but this study of the farm problem was necessary as background and for better understanding of the grim problem that lies ahead.

Table 3-1
ECONOMIC DECLINE OF THE AMERICAN FARMER
(Dollar Amounts in Billions. Number of Farms in Millions)

Year	Parity Ratio	Farm Debt	Number of Farms	Government Subsidies	Net Farm Income	Real Farm Income (1957-59 Dollars)
1945	109	$ 7.2	6.0	$0	$15.3	18.4
1950	101	12.4	5.6	.3	13.7	16.3
1955	84	17.6	4.6	.2	11.5	12.2
1960	80	24.9	4.0	.7	12.0	11.6
1965	77	39.3	3.3	2.5	15.1	13.7
1970	72	59.0	2.9	3.7	16.9	12.5

4

THE FOOD PROBLEM

> There is failure here that topples all our success. . . .
> Children dying of pellegra must die because a profit can-
> not be taken from an orange. And coroners must fill in the
> certificates—died of malnutrition—because food must rot,
> must be forced to rot.
>
> JOHN STEINBECK
> *The Grapes of Wrath*

Did you read John Steinbeck's famous novel *The Grapes of Wrath*? And did you know that, even though it is a "novel," it was based on an actual study made by a social scientist? If your answer to either question is *no*, you are about to meet a problem you have never met before: the food problem.

In the preceding chapter we examined a surprising fact: farmers tend to produce more when they are paid less! However, there were logical reasons why this should be so, and much statistical evidence to show that it is so. We found it surprising only because we are so much more familiar with the way industry operates: industry produces less when it is paid less.

Now, it will be recalled that in earlier chapters we examined a very awkward arrangement: prosperity prevails only when there are continuing substantial increases in the debt that is owed, and, when this debt ceases to expand, depression ensues, loosing the forces that cause industry to reduce production. But these forces are also the very ones that cause farmers to strive to *increase* production.

The most sensational case of failure of debt to expand and, therefore, depression, was the crash of 1929-32. So, if we want to illustrate this strange contrast between industrial output and farm output in time of contracting credit, we would choose that period. Below, in Table 4-1, are those data pertinent to the matter of the food problem.

Table 4-1

Year	(1) Parity Ratio (1910-14=100)	(2) Farm Production (1935-39=100)	(3) Industrial Production (1935-39=100)
1929	89	101	110
1930	80	98	91
1931	64	105	75
1932	55	102	58

Column 2 of the table shows the tendency for farm output to increase even under the most unfavorable economic conditions. The 1% increase from 1929 to 1932 can be seen directly. The slight decline (3 percentage points) from 1929 to 1930 resulted mainly from the terrible dust storms of that period. Even so, average farm production for the three depression years 1930-32 slightly exceeds the rate for 1929. Obviously there is no "food problem" so far as farm output is concerned.

The food problem is to be seen in Column 3, industrial production. Here we see a production decline of 47% from 1929 to 1932. Industry makes matches, for example, but it also makes margarine. Industry produces iron, tin and cans, but it also produces canned vegetables and fruits. You can think of many important food items that you recognize as being more the products of industry than of agriculture. If industry curtails output, and part of this output is food, then the amount of food available for consumption is reduced. *This* is the food problem. And Column 3 makes it obvious that this problem existed to some extent in 1930-32.

In Figure 2 the data for farm production and industrial production are graphed for the period 1920-40. This is the *basic* graph that shows the problem in a general overall way. This is the base from which the argument takes off, so to speak. Actually, these two sets of gross figures—aggregate output in the two categories—are too fuzzy for a detailed study of the single matter: food production. For example, farm production includes cotton, tobacco and other non-food products. And manufactured food items are only a very small part of total industrial production. In 1929, for example, food and kindred products amounted to only 10% of all manufacturing, and the latter was only a part of over-all industrial production. But the basic message in the graph—industrial production fell 47% while farm production increased 1%—should be borne in mind.

This 47% drop in industrial production is, in itself, an overall *average*. If we examine it in more detail we find, for example, that iron and steel output from 1929 through 1932 declined by 76%. And the output of transportation equipment (e.g., automobiles) dropped 71%. It should be noted that these two classes of industry are highly monopolized—that is, steel and automobiles were made by really giant corporations even in 1929. On the other hand, textile output declined only 24%, and leather products fell only 20%. Both of these latter classes of industry were not so highly monopolized as were automobiles and steel.

The class of industry—"food and kindred products"—most important to the food problem recorded a 22% decline in output from 1929 through 32. This decline of almost one-fourth is another startling, and more direct, bit of evidence of the existence of a food problem in 1932. But, again, so general a class of industry does not lend itself to detailed study.

The *particular* setting of the food problem lies in the difference between competitive production and monopolistic production *of food*. In a time of contracting debt, the former will tend to increase; the latter will decline. If, for example, chickens were grown by many small producers but turkeys were grown by a few large producers, then, in a time of depression, chicken production would increase while turkey production would decline. This is exactly the sort of thing that happened to butter and margarine production in 1929-32.

In many ways butter and margarine are quite similar. Indeed, scientific tests have shown that many people cannot taste the difference. Also the food values of both are practically identical.

FIGURE 2

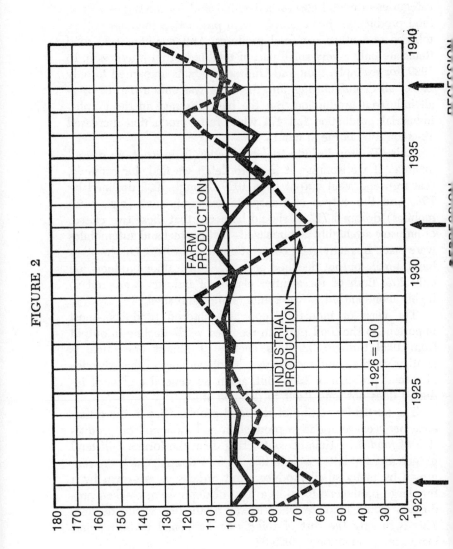

But the economic *sizes* of the producers of the two items are quite different. In 1929, there were 3,527 creameries plus a large number of farms that made butter. But margarine was made by only 41 establishments.

There is, however, another significant difference between these two food items: margarine is much cheaper than butter. So, common sense would tell us that, in time of depression, with unemployment high and incomes low, people in general would wish to consume less butter and more margarine in order to stretch their food budgets. But the economic theory we are here pursuing would tell us just the opposite: it would tell us that people would have to *reduce* their consumption of margarine because its production would be reduced. And they would have to do this despite their desire for cheaper food. At this point we had better look at the facts.

The production figures for margarine and butter are not too difficult to come by. They show that, from 1929 to 1932, the production of margarine decreased from 333,000,000 pounds to 215,000,000 pounds. This was a drop of over 35%.

As to butter: In 1929, production of butter totaled 2,160,000,-000 pounds. By 1932, the annual production was up to 2,276,000,-000 pounds. This was an increase of over 5%.

So, the paradox is real. During the depth of a great depression, people consumed *more butter and less margarine* than they did during the top year of the boom. And they did this in spite of the fact that margarine cost only half as much as butter.[1]

Further study will show that the food problem is real, too. In food quantity, the 35% drop in margarine overbalanced the 5% increase in butter. The net result was a loss in apparent civilian consumption of the combined products of over half a pound per person, or 3%. That is, the average amount of butter plus margarine consumed per person was 3% less in 1932 than in 1929. You know that people didn't *want* to eat less of these things in 1932. It was *necessary* because margarine output was 35% less in 1932 than in 1929. Here, then, is the crux of the food problem.

---

[1]In 1932, wholesale. See *Business Statistics,* 1947 edition, pp. 127, 133.

The production figures for margarine and butter are graphed in Figure 3. The line graphs in this particular case show the indexes of production on a per capita basis. You see, the total output of any food item is not nearly so important as the output per person. The consumption of food in China might be greater than in the United States. But the consumption per Chinaman would be another matter. Actually, all production figures (indexes of physical volume) are more informative when reduced to a per person basis. In either event, however, a comparison of the graphs in Figures 2 and 3 will show that:

1. The ups and downs of margarine production are quite similar to the ups and downs of industrial production.

2. Butter production is steady and tends to rise in depressions just as does overall farm production.

So, it is really true that the production of margarine—just as with most other products of big industry—is reduced when debt fails to increase. And this is so despite the wants of the people or their need for food. Margarine, it appears, is not really a cheap substitute for butter. It is a luxury which, like automobiles and steel, we consume in large amounts only when we are going rapidly into debt. If we stop going into debt, production is reduced. As a necessary consequence, consumption must be reduced, too.

Let us pursue this line of study further. Let us next examine the production figures for canned vegetables vs. fresh vegetables. We are all aware that a small number of large canning companies produce most of our canned vegetables. And we know that only a few corporations make the cans. On the other hand, we know that a great number of small truck farmers are engaged in raising fresh vegetables. We also know, for example, that a small potato farmer can get his spuds to market without the Intercontinental Can Corporation getting in on the act.

Vegetable production figures are graphed in Figure 4. These line graphs are plotted directly from the production indexes listed in Table 4-2 at the end of the chapter; that is, they are not corrected for the increase in population. However, correcting the data to a per capita basis would make the depression drop in

FIGURE 3

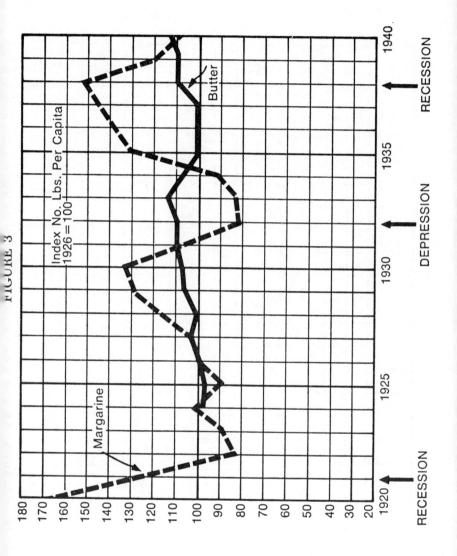

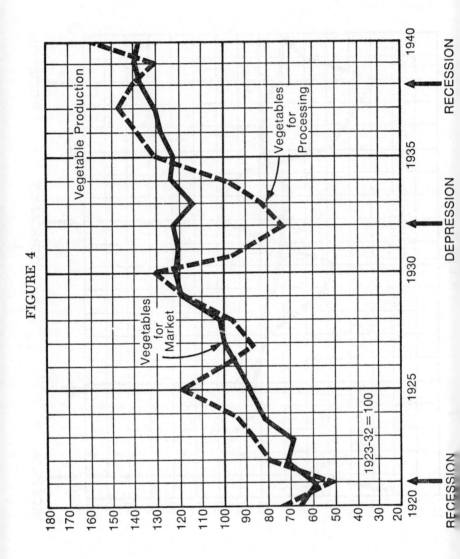

FIGURE 4

80

output of vegetables for processing look even worse. As it is, the figures show that the output of processed vegetables, the products of big business, dropped 44% from 1930 to 1932. This comes very near to matching the depression decline of 47% in overall industrial production as shown in Figure 2.

Once more, competitive production shows an increase in the face of contracting credit. The output of vegetables for market increased 2½% from 1929 to 1932. But again it turned out that the increase in competitive production failed to balance the drop in monopolistic production. The per capita loss of canned vegetables was about 7 pounds. The per capita gain of fresh vegetables was about 4 pounds. Net loss: 3 pounds of vegetables per person.

Next, let us consider canned pineapple. Only about eight corporations were engaged in growing and canning this product. For comparison, production figures are available for thirteen (other) fruits. That is, we will compare the monopolistic production of canned pineapple with the competitive production of native-grown fresh fruits. These production data are graphed in Figure 5. It will be noted on the graph that the production figures for both categories are more erratic than their counterparts in the preceding graphs. For one thing, native fruit crops vary from year to year because of the weather. For another, the eight corporations that controlled the pineapple industry also owned the plantations. So, if pineapples were to be left to rot in the fields it would be the corporation's pineapple.

Even so, the production figures show that (1) fresh fruit production increased 16% from 1929 to 1932; (2) canned pineapple production dropped 50% in the same period. Worse yet, the pineapple pack production data indicate that probably over 60% of the normal crop was left unpacked in the 1932-33 canning season. This can be deduced from the figures for pineapple pack listed in Column F of Table 4-2.

We have now examined in detail three particular cases illustrating the food problem in action: margarine vs. butter; processed vs. fresh vegetables; canned pineapple vs. fresh fruits. But these are not the only examples that can be found. Actually, the

FIGURE 5

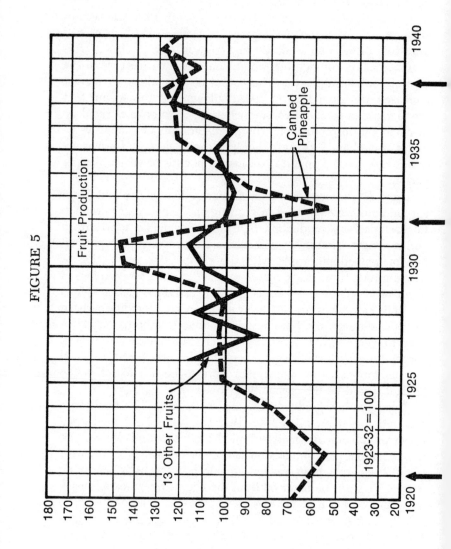

great credit contraction of 1929-32 produced many other cases. For example, milk produced on farms increased 5%, but ice cream production dropped 41%. Corn production increased 37%, but the production of corn cereal products decreased. Sheep production increased 1%. But wool consumed in manufacturing dropped 37%.

Let there be no doubt, there *was* a food problem in 1932. The output of manufactured food products, as a whole, dropped 22% from 1929. Furthermore, despite the increased production by small farmers, the food energy consumption per person was 6% lower in 1932 than it was in 1929.

There are many other series of data that confirm the trend shown by the ones discussed so far. Mostly, the production figures behave just as the theory of the food problem says they should behave. Listed below are changes in production (or apparent consumption) of other items for the period 1929 to 1932. You will be able to tell the monopolistic-enterprise product from the competitive-enterprise product without difficulty.

Beef Production (E-127)*	increased 12%
Canned Sardines (F-206)	dropped 73%
Hog Production (E-130)	increased 5%
Frozen Fish (F-199)	dropped 24%
Poultry Consumption (C-151)	increased 1.2%
Canned Salmon (F-202)	dropped 16%
Irish Potatoes (E-229)	increased 16%
Wheat Flour (C-153)	dropped 9%
Sweet Potatoes (E-229)	increased 32%
Cotton Consumed in Manufacturing (J-179)	dropped 30%

*Series and column number, *Historical Statistics of the United States, 1789-1945* (Washington, D.C., 1949).

All these are established facts. They cannot be refuted. They cannot be laughed off. They are disturbing, perhaps a bit frightening. They clearly show that our big business food manufacturers let us down badly in the early years of the last depression. But that was only the beginning of the food problem. It is true that a drop of 6% per person in available food energy was a sharp beginning. Nevertheless, it was only the beginning.

The crux of this matter is this:

1. When debt fails to increase and depression ensues, small enterprisers, such as farmers, increase their output.

2. Under the same conditions, big business reduces production. And the bigger, more concentrated the big business is, the more its production is reduced.

3. Conclusion: The food problem becomes more dangerous as big food manufacturers get bigger and less numerous. And the food problem gets potentially worse as the small food producers get bigger and less numerous.

Indeed, even with other things staying the same, the food problem can become more dangerous if the population increases, becomes more dependent upon manufactured food, and shifts from the country to urban areas where land for garden food-plots is lacking. So you can see at once why the food problem of the early thirties was only the beginning. In the succeeding decades these general changes, which would make the food problem more dangerous, have inexorably occurred. From 1930 to 1970, our population increased by 65%—an increase of more than 80,000,000 persons. Worse yet, in the same period, the portion of this population that is classed as urban increased from 56% to 70%. Further, the dependency on manufactured food has grown strikingly. Based upon their weight in the national income accounts, manufactured food and kindred products were only 25% as important as all farming in 1929; by 1970 they were 85% as important as farming.

When we turn from the general to the particular we find a similarly discouraging trend. Consider the change in the case of margarine vs. butter. In 1929 we used only one-sixth as much margarine as butter. So, when by 1932 margarine production had dropped by 35% and butter production had increased 5%, the net food loss for the combined products was only 3%. But by 1970 we were using twice as much margarine as butter. If, under these 1970 conditions, we assume similar production changes as occurred in 1929-32, we would calculate a potential net loss of food value of 22% had a great depression occurred in the early 1970s.

Unfortunately, other changes make the potential danger even worse. The production of both margarine and butter has become more monopolized since 1929. For margarine, the 41 establishments of 1929 had concentrated to 33 as early as 1954. During the same period the number of creameries decreased from 3,527 to only 1,262. By 1967 both industries had become even more monopolized: less than 20 companies made 97% of the margarine; only 510 companies were producing creamery butter, and the 50 largest of these accounted for 60% of the total output.

What about vegetables? In 1929-32, processed vegetables decreased 44%. At that time there were 2,997 canning and preserving establishments. But the 1947 census of manufactures showed only 2,265 establishments and only 1,856 companies. The 1967 census showed the continuing concentration: only 50 canning companies were producing 70% of the total output of canned fruits and vegetables.

From 1929 to 1967, the cereal-preparations establishments decreased from 121 to 45. By the early 1970s only 4 firms controlled 90% of the breakfast cereal market. So, one depression day, corn-flakes may be a luxury that only the rich can buy, the rest of us eating the corn just as it comes from the cob.

During the 1929-67 period, bakeries declined in number from 20,778 to 4,042. The 1967 census of manufactures showed that the top 20 baking companies were supplying 47% of the country's bread and related products; about the same concentration ratio as in paint manufacturing. The top 20 flour and meal companies were supplying 70% of the industry total. So, the monopolists are baking your bread. One depression day when you have no bread don't think you will eat cake. The monopolists bake that, too.

If you are thinking you could switch to beer, forget it. By 1975 the 5 largest beer companies had monopolized about two-thirds of the market.

Nor is there good news for the kiddies. From 1929 to 1932, ice cream production decreased 41%. But from 1929 to 1954 the number of ice cream producing establishments was reduced by 50%. By 1967, the top 20 companies in the ice cream industry had cornered 60% of the market; actually a higher degree of concentration than that in the aluminum castings industry.

If we hoped to find some good news we would seek it among the farmers: those competitive enterprisers who produced more when they were paid less. In the early 1930s the farmers increased food output at the most critical time: when the monopolists decreased their output of food. As recounted before, the industrial food manufacturers reduced output but the farmers increased their output so that the net loss in food per person was only 6%.

Unfortunately, there is no longer basis for hope that the family-size farms can save us from the monopolists again. The trend toward concentration that we noted among the food manufacturers also affects our agricultural land. In 1920, over three-quarters of all land in farms was in parcels of less than 500 acres; less than one-quarter was in parcels 1,000 acres and up. But by 1969, over half of all land in farms was in holdings greater than 1,000 acres. Actually by the early 1970s nearly half the land in farms was in holdings 2,000 acres and over. These are not family-sized farms. Their *average* size is over 7,500 acres or nearly 12 square miles. These are "factories in the fields."

In the table below you can follow the trend away from competitive enterprise family-size farms and the trend toward factory-size farms.

Size of Farm (Acres)	Percent Distribution of All Land in Farms					
	1920	1930	1940	1950	1959	1969
100-499	49	45	42	36	32	27
1,000 and over	23	28	34	43	49	54

Source: Table No. 968, p. 586, *Statistical Abstract of the United States,* 1972 and prior issues.

Ever since we became a nation one of our democratic ideals has been that agricultural land should be owned in family-sized units by those who till the soil. Periodically this political philosophy has blossomed into a national land policy, most notably in the Homestead Act of 1862. Homesteads were set at one-quarter square mile each.

The change from that democratic ideal of the 1860s to the economic actualities of the 1970s measures our departure from basic ideals. For 25 years, 1950-75, the smaller and family-sized farms were eliminated at an average rate of more than 10,000 each month. By 1975 the top 5% of the farms made over 50% of total farm sales; more than half of the land under cultivation in California was corporate-owned; and a new "farm" in North Carolina embraced 585 square miles—the equivalent of over two thousand homesteads. So, farms still are becoming larger and less numerous, and it should be obvious that this tide of events continues to add to the potential severity of the food problem.

Theoretically, then, the food problem will eventually result in a terrible disaster: starvation in the midst of potential plenty. To alert us to this danger, we have only a long-forgotten precedent—and a novel, *The Grapes of Wrath*. So, it may come upon us without much warning. All the trends are working against us. The ill-fated drift of the defective economy that got us into this mess gets us in deeper every day. The concentration of ownership of industry, including food manufacturing, goes on at a frightening pace. The owner-operated family-size farms continue to disappear—devoured by factories-in-the-fields. The number of us potential victims keeps increasing by more than two million a year. None of these unfavorable trends can be readily stopped, let alone reversed. Moreover, all of these circumstances would have to be put back to the status of about 1920 in order for us to be safe from the food problem.

History shows that disasters tend to be especially damaging when common belief at the time held them to be impossible: the "unsinkable" *Titanic*, for example. The first step in dealing with this food problem is to recognize its potentiality for disrupting the food supply and the probability of its happening. Once the danger is recognized there is a possible way to prevent the problem from causing too much havoc: minimum production quotas could be set for all corporate farms and food manufacturers. Each food corporation could be monitored so that any dangerous reduction in our food supply could be prevented. Of course, enabling legislation complete with enforcement provisions and adequate manpower would be required. To be practicable some provisions would be required for reimbursing the corporations for any financial loss that might occur. Frankly, there are few corporations that would work to feed the hungry unless there was some money in it.

Table 4-2

Year	(A) Creamery Butter Manufacture (Million Pounds)	(B) Oleomargarine Production (Million Pounds)	(C) Production Index (17 Vegetables for Market)	(D) Production Index (8 Vegetables for Processing)	(E) Production Index (13 Fruits)	(F) Pineapple Pack (1000 Cases)
1920		391	64	75	85	5,987
1921		281	58	50	61	5,262
1922		190	72	81	49	4,770
1923		209	63	86	96	5,895
1924	1,357	239	82	95	88	6,825
1925	1,363	215	88	129	88	8,728
1926	1,464	248	89	97	110	8,940
1927	1,498	257	98	85	87	8,879
1928	1,488	294	101	95	115	8,663
1929	1,597	333	119	117	87	9,210
1930	1,638	249	121	132	109	12,672
1931	1,680	277	119	91	117	12,807
1932	1,694	215	122	74	101	
1933	1,763	219	113	80	98	4,657*
1934	1,694	243	124	99	99	7,985
1935	1,632	353	122	130	105	9,478
1936	1,629	372	128	125	94	10,636
1937	1,624	389	129	147	125	10,796
1938	1,786	415	136	142	119	11,353
1939	1,782	332	140	127	125	9,708
1940	1,872	304	138	158	126	11,370

*Pack year.

Sources:

Column A: Table, "Dairy Products Manufactured," *Statistical Abstract of the United States*, 1946, 1941, 1938, 1931.

Column B: Table 796, "Oleomargarine Production, Total," *ibid.*, 1949 (1941).

Columns C, D: Table 726, "Crop Production," *ibid.*, 1949.

Column E: *Ibid.*

Column E: Table 705, "Crop Production," *ibid.*, 1941.

Column F: *Western Canner and Packer Year Book*, 1920 to 1931 (Pineapple Producers Cooperative Association 1932-33 to 1939-40).

5

THE RESOURCE
DESTRUCTION MOTIVE

If consumption exceeds production, the capital of the
country must be diminished, and its wealth must be gradually destroyed from its want of power to produce.

Thomas Robert Malthus
Principles of Political Economy

Near Louisville, one day in 1813, a man named Audubon saw
an astounding sight: a flight of passenger pigeons so vast that it
darkened the sky. He estimated that this single flock—a mile wide
and 180 miles long—contained more than one billion birds.

It is believed that the passenger pigeon may have been the
most impressive species of bird that mankind has ever known.
So elegant, graceful and swift, they were called "blue meteors."
Truly an American species, they inhabited the eastern half of the
United States and southeastern Canada in numbers estimated to
total between three billion and six billion birds. They migrated
and nested in such enormous flocks as to tax the observer's belief.
Audubon was a young man of twenty-three when he saw the
billion-bird flock. He lived none too soon to see such sights.

During Audubon's lifetime, passenger pigeons were killed for
food and sold in the marketplace for that purpose. In the early
eighteen hundreds, the going retail price was about 12¢ per
dozen. But in 1851, the year of Audubon's death, 150,000 dozen
pigeons were sent to market from a single nesting near Platts-
burgh, New York. The market price at the time was about 56¢
per dozen.

By 1861, several railroad lines had reached the Mississippi,
a transcontinental telegraph system was complete, and the

slaughter and sale of wild pigeons had become a big business. Shipments of birds to market were made by railway express. The express companies made so much money from this business that their agents kept the commercial trappers informed by telegraph about the movement of the flocks. This was done year-round, and the agents tried not to overlook a single flock or a single nesting.

During the 1860s, nets were developed that could trap up to 3,500 birds at a time. Worse yet, the market demand was growing for "squabs"—the young passenger pigeons that were taken from their nests before they could fly. In 1874, two million pounds of squabs (plus 200,000 dozen adult birds) were sent to market from the Michigan nestings alone. The price by that time had risen to $2.50 per dozen.

At Petosky, Michigan, in 1878, the last really huge nesting was practically wiped out. An estimated two thousand people, including Indians working for hire, engaged in the harvesting operations. The killing continued from March 22 until August 12, almost five months. Earnings up to $40 a day were made by the "pigeoneers," and one of those working this nesting was reported to be worth $60,000, all made in this single business. Despite conflicting reports, it appears that a hundred million pigeons were killed at this one nesting area alone. The destruction was so furious and widespread that no one could keep count. Later, much smaller nestings were easier to assess. In 1882, over two million birds were killed in Wisconsin, including almost all the squabs in the nesting. The price by 1882 had risen to $3.50 per dozen. This was the end of the important nestings of the species. By 1900, only occasional single birds were being shot. In 1903, the last wild passenger pigeon was taken—and this dirty business was at an end.

A few passenger pigeons, however, still lingered on in captivity. These gradually died off until only one, named Martha, remained alive in the Cincinnati zoo. Near the end of the summer of 1914 the final extinction of this once great species was near: Martha was dying of old age. Sometime during the afternoon of September 1, her lifeless body was found on the ground in her pen. Martha was then frozen in a cake of ice and shipped to the Smithsonian Institution. How merciful that Audubon could not witness this cold and bitter ending of so glorious a species. The enormity of its extinction was given expression by William Beebe, who wrote: "When a race of living things breathes no more, another heaven and earth must pass before such a one can be again."

The fate of the passenger pigeon is probably history's most sensational case of extermination of a species. And it wasn't just an accident. The nearly similar fate of the American bison discounts this possibility. The bison was America's most impressive species of mammal: a magnificent animal standing six feet high at the shoulders and weighing up to three thousand pounds. It is believed that sixty million of these "buffaloes" once roamed the unspoiled land of North America. As late as 1830 there were an estimated forty million of them living on the plains and prairie land, mostly west of the Mississippi. As meat alone (which was considered as good as that of domestic beef), they represented a greater quantity than now carried by all the beef cattle living in the same area. About 1850, a full-grown buffalo carefully worked up into its salable products—tongue, meat, tallow and robe—would fetch about $5. Obviously, a substantial industry could be supported by forty million bison worth $5 apiece.

"The period of systematic slaughter," wrote Dr. W. T. Hornaday, "naturally begins with the first organized effort in a businesslike wholesale way." Perfection of the breech-loading rifle, and the building of railroads into the main bison area, permitted such operations to begin. In 1869, the Union Pacific Railroad was completed, effectively dividing the great herds into two parts. Worse yet, this railroad and two others (the Santa Fe and the Kansas Pacific) made the southern herds commercially accessible to eastern markets. Depots were established. Warehouses for meat and hides were built. Merchants set up shops for the sale of provisions, the breech-loading rifles and suitable ammunition. After these commercially necessary preliminaries, bison-killing, as a big business, got underway. From 1870 through 1875 the slaughter averaged at least 2,500,000 bison per year. During this period, robes brought about $1.25 apiece. Buffalo tongues were 25¢ to 50¢ each; meat brought up to 5¢ a pound; and a new product—bones for fertilizer and charcoal—brought from $7 to $10 per ton.

Soon over 5,000 men were occupied just in the slaughter end of the business. A good rifleman could kill a hundred bison in a day; over 1,500 in a season. The individual record was 3,000 bison in 30 days. Dr. Hornaday's 1887 Smithsonian Report included the following description of production methods:

> A cordon of camps was established along the Arkansas River, the South Platte, the Republican, and the few other streams that contained water, and when the thirsty animals came to drink they were attacked and driven away, and with the most fiendish persistency kept from slaking their thirst so that they would again be compelled to seek the river and come within the range of the deadly breechloaders.

By the end of 1876, business had fallen off in the southern area due to the lack of bison. But in 1880, the Northern Pacific Railroad was completed, making the northern herds commercially accessible. And the average price for robes had now risen to above $5: a 400% increase in less than ten years. So, the work force transferred operations to the north. Here the industry was prosecuted for another nine years. By 1889 the business was finished: less than a thousand bison remained alive in the entire country. Later, Henry Inman (*The Old Santa Fe Trail*, New York, 1898) working from an estimated total paid out for bones, believed he had accounted for the skeletons of over thirty-one million bison. Whatever the true total kill may have been, the American buffalo, as a free wild species, had ceased to exist.

Many parallels can be noted between the case of the passenger pigeon and that of the American bison. But the most glaring common aspect is that in each case an apparently inexhaustible resource—forty million bison and five billion passenger pigeons—had been destroyed in a relatively short period of time. Both were magnificent species of great use to mankind. Then suddenly they were gone, their usefulness ended, their value to mankind erased. After the bison were gone, many of our western Indians, who had depended upon them for food, died of starvation. With the extinction of the passenger pigeon, a thing of great beauty was lost to the world forever.

It is not surprising then that there has been much gloomy speculation as to just what it was that hit these innocent creatures. These forms of life were the triumphant products of thousands of centuries of successful struggle with the forces of nature. Then suddenly they were struck by a force they could not withstand. And it was clear that this deadly force had something to do with man, and man's way of doing business.

These creatures were the victims of a destructive coincidence: the misalliance of (1) man's love for money, (2) the rapid growth of modern industrialism, and (3) two strangely contradictory economic laws of the marketplace that determine price. Of these three things that combine to make this destructive force, it is only the price laws, and the role they play, that are little known. Certainly most Americans are familiar with man's love for money, and with the power of modern industrialism.

Most Americans, too, are familiar enough with the law of supply and demand to be fully aware that scarce things command a higher price than do things that are plentiful; and that the scarcer a thing is, the higher is its price. It is well known that widespread failure of some fruit or vegetable crop will cause the market price to rise. It is known too that when farmers raise a bumper crop of wheat or cotton, the prices for these things will fall. A common way of stating this proposition is to say that the greater the supply, the lower the price; and the less the supply, the higher the price. In other words, supply and price vary *inversely*.

On the other hand, at least when you stop to think of it a bit, it is nothing new to say that when prices rise, production also rises. Indeed it is well known that when prices are high, production likewise is high, and vice versa. For example, in 1929, when the price index stood at 95, the index of industrial production was 115. Three years later, when the price index had fallen to 65, the index of industrial production had fallen to 61. All who lived through the great depression know that prices were low and that production was low, too; and that during the subsequent boom when prices were high, production also was high. In the early postwar years, 1946-1951, when prices rose from 121 to 180, industrial production rose from 170 to 220. So it can be said that the higher the price, the greater the supply; and the lower the price, the less the supply. In other words, supply and price vary *directly*.

Now, it will be noted that in the two preceding paragraphs quite opposite statements have been made, and that both of them obviously are true. This is not just a trick of logic or of statistics. The two propositions *are* mathematically opposite, yet both are valid. Consider this: if you were to drive through the countryside and see farmers harvesting great quantities of corn, you may be sure the price of corn is low. When you enter the suburbs and observe that many new houses are being built, you may be quite sure that their price is high. Then as you pass the city markets and see large quantities of sea trout for sale you may be sure they are cheap. But when you pass a factory working full blast, three shifts a day, producing great numbers of automobiles, it is a safe bet that they are high in price. So you see, the two different price laws can be in evidence at the same time because each is dominating the price of different commodities. This explains how it is possible for both opposite propositions to be true and coexist in our everyday economic life.

That scarce things tend to be high in price, and plentiful things tend to be cheap, is a natural law of economics in the broadest sense. It is not known just when this old law of supply and demand was first noticed. But Charlemagne passed a law against it in the eighth century, and Adam Smith explained it fully in 1776. As a force in determining price, this old law has been in effect, no doubt, ever since trade began.

That high prices tend to bring on an increase in production, and that low prices tend to depress production, is a condition associated chiefly with industrialism under the profit motive. It was first described by John Stuart Mill little more than a hundred years ago. The human desire to acquire profits is very strong;

the power of modern industry is amazingly responsive. So, if a high market price prevails for the products of industry, the owners of industry *will* supply the market. The means of production are at their command; high prices for their products provide the incentive. Conversely, if prices are low the owners of industry slow down the rate of output. Modern industry is depressed by low, or falling, prices. For most of the things produced by industry and sold in the marketplace—bottle caps, air conditioners and motor buses, for example—this newer price system actually works in a satisfactory manner.

However, for those basic things that industry doesn't produce but only brings to market, *both* of these contradictory price laws apply in a peculiarly destructive manner. For example, suppose there is a demand for sealskin coats. By modern industrial means, fur seals can be caught, skinned, transported, tanned, sewed into coats, advertised and sold, quite profitably. But industry *does not produce the seals.* Industry, in the act of supplying the market, succeeds only in *reducing* the number of seals—the source of supply of sealskin coats. This reduction in supply will cause a relative scarcity which, assuming only that the demand holds up, will cause a rise in price in the marketplace. The higher price will increase the incentive. So, industry will try harder to supply the market. In the effort, the basic supply of seals once more will be reduced. So, the price once again will rise. And once more the seals will be reduced in number. Unless acted upon by some influence outside of the marketplace, inevitably the very last fur seal in existence will be caught and brought to market; and sold at a very high price.

Consider the underlying process closely: a reduction in basic supply will bring about a rise in the market price; this rise in price will spur industry to exert greater effort to supply the market; and this will further reduce the basic supply. Thus it is a snowballing sequence of economic events that drives inexorably toward the destruction of nature's goods. Forests, fur-bearers, fish, wildlife, ores, petroleum—*all those things that are uniquely nature's and that are harvested for profit without restriction, in-evitably—because of a deadly coincidence of powerful economic forces—will be destroyed.* This, then, in all its terrible simplicity is the resource destruction motive: man's inherent greed for gain, the power of modern industrialism, and the irresistible price laws of the marketplace combining to form what is probably the single most destructive force ever known.

Of these various economic forces that combine to make up this motive, industrialism was perhaps the latest one to develop—the straw that broke the camel's back, so to speak. This part of the destructive coincidence, in America at least, came of age in the 1850 decade or, at the very latest, by 1865. Even prior to this, however, there were occasional examples of the resource destruction motive in action. Usually these cases applied to natural commodities that did not require modern industrial methods to get them to market. One such was the great auk: an unwary creature that permitted himself to be clubbed and harvested without the use of elaborate equipment. So, his numbers dwindled. As they grew scarcer, the going price for skins, and even for eggs, rose to an attractive figure: up to $40 for a skin and $1 for an egg. This attracted purchasing agents to set up in likely places—Iceland for example—and bid for the birds on both spot and future basis. Thus, a particular commercial significance was assigned to the remnants of the species. It was simply a matter of good business for every sealing or fishing expedition to keep an eye open for the remaining auks.

All the great auks were exterminated by 1844. But the prices continued to rise even after the auks were extinct. In 1868 a specimen was sold to the American Museum of Natural History for $625. In 1881 an Englishman paid over $1000 for two eggs; then bought another in 1883 for $700. Thus the resource destruction motive continued to operate even after the basic resource had been destroyed.

The unfortunate auks, by submitting to the irresistible pressure of a rising price so early as 1844, escaped a fate that would have been even more violent. The treatment they received from the commercial market was almost gentle compared with that given the American bison. Of course, the bison furnished more marketable products than did the poor auk. So, a greater number and variety of merchants were attracted to the business. But the most important difference was the more advanced state of industrial methods.

Actually, the post-mortem operation of the resource destruction motive—noted just above in the case of the poor auks—almost finished off the bison. As recounted earlier, bison slaughter, as a big business, ended in 1889, when less than a thousand of them remained alive. But during the 1890s the price continued to rise. Taxidermists would pay up to $300 for a bison head delivered to their shops. The record price reported paid for a single head was $1,500. Such prices made it profitable to hunt down the surviving buffaloes one by one. This is exactly what happened to the Lost Park herd in Colorado. The last four of these were killed in 1897. This left as the only wild "herd" a pitiful twenty-one bison in Yellowstone National Park. At this point the forces of government finally got the business stopped.

But the resource destruction motive wasn't stopped. There were other commodities of nature in demand in the marketplace: sea-otter furs, for example. Prior to the United States purchase of Alaska in 1867, the previous owners had been taking only 700 sea-otter skins annually. These furs brought about $150 apiece on the market. After 1867, in typically industrious fashion, American enterprise soon increased the harvest rate to 4,000 skins. Later, with the business better organized under the Alaska Commercial Company, the annual harvest was increased to about 5,000 skins. But by 1900, only 33 years after we bought Alaska, the catch was down to only 127 skins. For the year 1910 the Company's entire fleet of ships caught less than three dozen otters. By then, the price of sea-otter pelts had risen to over $1,700 apiece. The less there were, the more they were worth. And the more they were worth, the scarcer they were made.

Still, there were other things uniquely nature's to be processed. And industry constantly improved its efficiency toward this purpose. As the century began, lumber prices were rising as our great forests receded. Lumber production, which in 1850 had been only about 5 billion board feet, was pushed to a peak of 46 billion board feet in 1906. So, the forests receded faster and the rate of cutting had to fall off. After that, the price rose at a faster rate. Although the price for lumber in the years that followed increased by 600%, and bulldozers and power chain saws were invented, cutting never again reached the 1906 rate. Some particularly desirable species, notably the eastern white pine and the black walnut, were commercially destroyed. By the late 1960s the black walnut was falling prey to the post-mortem syndrome: "tree rustlers" were actively stealing them one by one from private walnut groves to supply a market that paid up to $500 for a single black walnut trunk.[1] Whether animals, birds, or trees, so long as the price went up, industry worked efficiently toward their extermination. So long as industry did this, the price inevitably went up.

Indeed, by the turn of the century, modern industrialism had become so effective and the resource destruction motive was operating so forcefully that even an obscure little South American animal, the chinchilla, found itself in serious trouble. The chinchilla was small, wary and quick. But he had a fatal defect: luscious, silvery fur. So, despite the remoteness of his habitat, he got caught in a rising fur market. As the price rose (and as the supply decreased) the furriers ordered their agents to buy skins at any price. In 1905, with the price about $8 apiece, the trappers caught nearly 220,000. Within four years the price had risen to $40 a skin, but the catch was down to less than 28,000. The Peruvian variety, the royal chinchilla, was practically exterminated. They are now virtually extinct. The Chilean variety was saved by government protection and has made something of a comeback.

Now, birds are small, wary and quick, too. But, in 1914, more than sixty different species were being killed, mainly for the millinery trade. One very beautiful American species, the Carolina parakeet, was exterminated. Both the snowy egret and the American egret were brought to the verge of extinction. In 1914, during a three-month period, 1,470 pounds of egret feathers were sold in the London market alone. These were used mainly

---

[1] By 1973 the price had risen to $1,500.

for *"aigretts"* for women's hats. About one hundred egrets had to be killed to supply a pound of feathers. Worse yet, since prime feathers were gathered during the nesting season, two or three young egrets starved in the nest for every adult egret whose feathers went to market. So, this three-month period represented the death of over 300,000 egrets. This destructive business, by the way, was motivated by high prices in the marketplace: egret feathers were then selling for about $800 a pound. A little arithmetic will show that the three months' sales resulting from the death of a third of a million egrets brought in over a million dollars to the people in the bird-feather trade.

Many of nature's things, in those early years of the century, were, or were close to becoming, business failures. But there was one benign animal that seemed to be able to hold its own. This was the harp seal of the northwestern Atlantic. Harvesting these began about 1750. But harp seals do not fur coats make: they are hair seals. So they were harvested only for oil and leather. No doubt the population over the years was reduced somewhat. But *Chafe's Sealing Book* shows the catch to have been fairly stable over a 26-year period, 1895-1919, at an average annual rate of about 200,000 seals. During this time the value to the market hunters stayed stable, too, averaging less than $2 per animal. So this wasn't a very large industrial enterprise: less than one-fourth the monetary importance of the business supported by the little chinchilla in 1905.

This long-term stable catch (and price) strongly suggests a stable population. Based on current knowledge the population must have averaged in excess of three and a half million seals. From 1919 to 1939, the harvest from this herd averaged only about 150,000 per year. During these years the sealing fleet was stabilized at about ten vessels. And the value was stable, too, remaining at $2 per carcass or less. During World War II men were so busy killing men that they eased up killing harp seals. Indeed the average catch, 1940 through 1948, was less than 65,000 per year. So, the harp seal population probably recovered to its nineteenth-century numbers.

To better understand what happens next we must examine

in more detail, both biological and economic, this uniquely nature's thing that we are dealing with. The western Atlantic herd is the most important of three distinct populations of harp seals. They live their lives in the arctic seas between Greenland and Canada. Each February, the females haul up on the edge of the new winter's ice east and west of Newfoundland. Here they bear their young: the "whitecoats." These thirty-pound bundles of snow-white loveliness are nursed by their mothers for about two weeks, during which the pups more than triple their weight to about a hundred pounds, of which (note this) over half is fat. These young are (note this) helpless except for the natural camouflage of their white coat. This white coat is not technically "fur." Rather, it is soft, thick, pure-white fetal hair, which (and note this) is "fast" to the hide for about a week. After two weeks the pups begin to shed and take on a black-blotched hair coat. No longer helpless whitecoats, and deserted by their mothers, they can enter the sea and are on their own.

But as whitecoats they possessed up to three commercial products: oil, leather and fur. The latter developed from new technologies, and demand for trim and specialty products such as slippers, belts and purses. Up to 1951 oil was the dominant product, later supplanted by the fur. But in all cases, the white-coat, not the adult seal, was the more desired natural raw material.

The whitecoats ever had been harvested by simply clubbing them to death in a businesslike manner. For two centuries this had been done on a sustained-yield basis. Then in the late 1940s the business picked up. By 1949 the catching effort was twice what it had been before the war. The old sealing fleet had been replaced with newer vessels. The Norwegian sealers used specially built diesel-powered ships. The Canadians used some special sealing ships plus ice-strengthened coastal ships. Aircraft were used to spot the herds.

In 1950-1951, scientific aerial surveys set the population for the entire herd at about three and three-quarter million. But in 1951, over 50% of the young of the year were killed: 340,000 taken out of a total crop of 645,000. In 1952 the catch was less but the value to the sealers was up to $3 each. In 1955, some Russian ships joined the hunt for the first time. And in 1956 a record number of whitecoats were slaughtered: 342,745. By 1959, the harvest was down again but the price was up to $4 per carcass. For the years 1949 through 1961 the annual harvest had averaged 225,000 whitecoats plus 85,000 olders seals. A second aerial census (1959-60) estimated the total stock at a million and a half, down by more than one-half since 1950. And in 1962 the value per carcass went above $5.

In 1961, the Russians sent an icebreaker to help their sealers. But in 1962 the Canadians leaped to the forefront by using helicopters to put the clubbers on the ice and take the dead, or dying, pups to the ship. In 1964, total kill (whitecoats plus adults) amounted to 325,000, including over 70% of the pups of the year. The average value of whitecoats had now soared to over $18 each, and the end of another thing uniquely nature's was in sight.

But not just yet! The harp seals had some friends the likes of which had not been available to the auks, the passenger pigeons, Carolina parakeets, bison or chinchillas. These invaluable friends were two Canadian scientists, Dr. H. D. Fisher and Dr. David Sergeant, and an enlightened Canadian government. The two scientists, calmly and with professional skill, measured the increasing harvest and declining population, and kept their government informed. With scientific thoroughness they studied every aspect of the seal herd: age distribution, birth rates, mortality rates of adults and young, breeding age, fertility, total population. They reported their findings at the North American Wildlife Conference; in the *Canadian Audubon;* in the British *Polar Record.* As a result of their work, the Canadian government imposed restrictions on the catch beginning in 1965.

After that, the Russian icebreakers went elsewhere (but not to their own depleted herd in the White Sea; they stopped all sealing there in 1964 for a period of five years). The Norwegians sent a ship in 1964-65 to look into the matter of the crabeater seals in the Antarctic. Very little is known about crabeater seals, or their past history. About their future we know very much: the fewer they become the more they will be worth; and the more that they are worth, the fewer they will become.

You see, the case of the harp seal brings us nearly down to date. It contradicts any idea, or propaganda, that the commercial market acquires a conscience with the passage of time. It does not. Nor does industry acquire wisdom or restraint. On the contrary, it acquires greater efficiency in its ability to destroy nature's goods. And man's greed for gain shows no improvement whatever.

True, the two Canadian scientists represent something new. But this one case does not prove a trend. An enlightened government that acts effectually is an improvement, too. But the scientists had proved, by 1961 at the latest, the need to restrict the catch. The restrictions did not take effect until 1965. During the three years' needless delay, a million seals were slaughtered. Even so, it does appear that the harp seals were saved in the nick of time, and the scientist-government team deserves the credit.

Contemporary with this notable Canadian triumph was a typically American tragedy. This tragedy concerns what at one time had been man's best friend: the horse. In principle it is all too typical, but there are some interesting differences. So, we will start at the very beginning.

In 1540, under Coronado, a Spanish expedition with over a thousand horses invaded what is now New Mexico. While the Spaniards were in winter quarters along the Rio Grande, Indian raiders drove off most of their horses. The Spaniards recaptured some, the Indians sequestered some, but some escaped into the countryside. In their Mexican stronghold to the south, the Spaniards had plenty of horses. So they kept trying to subjugate the Indians and lost more horses in the process. The Spanish abandoned New Mexico in 1680, leaving behind almost all their stock. By then, of course, the Indians had horses. And America had wild horses: the mustangs.

Very fine horses they were too. They had come from Andalusia out of stock whose lineage went back to North Africa and Arabia. An Englishman, encountering these famous horses in

Spain, wrote that they were "strangely wise, beyond any man's imagination." For the long rigorous voyage from Spain to Mexico, the Spaniards selected only the strongest horses; only the strongest of these survived the passage.

No doubt only the most spirited and intelligent of these were the ones to grasp the chance for freedom in the virgin expanse of western America. Here they found a home surprisingly home-like. In soil and terrain it was similar to the arid lands from which their race had sprung. They prospered and multiplied. By 1700, Spanish-type horses were seen as far north as Saskatchewan. By 1800, herds of wild horses with five thousand head or more were quite common. At their peak, about 1850, they may have numbered up to five million scattered over an area of a million and a half square miles.

The American mustang was a fine animal and a wild one. (It is important to understand this, for later, when the mustang met a fate so ignoble as to be obscene, the businessmen and government men both swore to the contrary.) During the nineteenth century, mustangs were in demand as riding horses. Lieutenant U. S. Grant rode one while campaigning in 1846. It took good men—the mustangers—to catch them, and the best of the mustangs did not get caught. Famous wild horses were given names that denoted respect: White Pacer, Black Devil, Blue Streak and Starface. The latter, when cornered by a group of mustangers, leaped off a cliff to certain death rather than submit to capture. They were wild enough, and fine and beautiful and free. Their chronicler, J. Frank Dobie, wrote that "the aesthetic value of the mustang topped all other values. The sight of wild horses streaming across the prairie made even the most hardened of professional mustangers regret putting an end to their liberty."

The years brought change. The demand for mustangs as riding and working animals fell off. The mustangers—capable of regrets—faded away, supplanted by more businesslike stockmen who grazed their cattle and sheep on the public domain. These practical men considered the mustang a predator that ate some public grass and drank some public water. From this arrangement the stockmen could derive no gain. On the contrary, they received only insult: the mustangs enticed away every unfettered domestic horse, sheepman's or cattleman's, that had a sense for the life of the free. This was the last straw. The stockmen scourged the mustangs: shot them, poisoned their waterholes. The mustangs had no protection under the law; they were not wildlife! They were called feral unbranded horses. By about 1930, the population of mustangs had been reduced to less than a million animals.

The years brought change elsewhere. The demand for *domestic* horses fell off, too. The tractor, the truck and the motorcar made them obsolescent. Domestic horses became surplus faster than the glue-men could use them up. Then an entrepreneur had an idea: horse meat for dog food. This idea gave birth to an industry that later consumed the mustang. Wartime scarcity and rationing of meat led dog owners to increase their demand for horse meat. The supply of domestic ex-workhorses could not keep up, and the industry turned to mustangs.

Processing plants were set up from Utah to California. Aircraft were used to drive the herds toward specially built corrals with outstretched wings. By 1948 the rate of harvest so taxed the local plants that a carload of wild horses was shipped all the way from western Montana to a cannery in eastern Kansas— 1,500 miles. The wholesale price at the canneries rose 100% from 1946 to 1952 and another 50% by 1956. And remember, horse meat had to compete with beef, chicken and domestic horse meat on price alone: to man's last remaining friend, the dog, the source of the meat was a matter of complete indifference.

So the hundreds of thousands of mustangs faded away. When they became too scarce to herd into corrals, the airplanes "spooked" the few survivors out of their canyon hiding places onto the open plain. Here they were run down one by one by men in trucks: mustangs tire; trucks do not.

There were, and are, Americans who would not be indifferent to all this, but they didn't know. The whole matter had been strictly a business proposition. Then in early 1957, a newspaper ran a story about what was happening to the mustangs in Nevada. Promptly the governor of Nevada was deluged with letters of protest, mostly from out-of-state. He replied by form letter stating that he opposed cruelty to animals, but it was the *counties* that permitted the business, not the state of Nevada! This was a pussyfoot excuse, but it was too late anyway. Only a few thousand Nevada mustangs remained uncanned. These were processed during the next few years. As of 1970, an estimated total of 15,000 mustangs of the original five million remained in the entire United States. Extermination was 99.7% complete.

Luckily, there was no post-mortem operation of the resource destruction motive on these few survivors. The dogs, without much complaint, resumed eating other things. So, no one bid up the price. However, there was a post-mortem pang of American conscience: in September 1959, Congress set up a $500 fine for poisoning waterholes or catching mustangs with airplanes or trucks on federal land (but it wasn't enforced).

If at this point the reader feels a twinge of shame it is forgivable. Any further emotion should be repressed. The resource destruction motive is an emotionless force. Its depredations may cause remorse, but remorse will never change it.

In principle, the resource destruction motive is simple and direct. In operation, however, there are many complexities, which are examined in the next chapter. The motive's victims—things uniquely nature's—can introduce their own complicating aspects. The examples used in this chapter are among the simplest and were further simplified in the telling.

Generally, a living resource, undisturbed, is in balance with nature. So, when its turn comes in the marketplace, its quantity soon declines and its price soon rises. Thus it starts on its way to extinction. But not with simple precision. Near the time of peak harvest of passenger pigeons, an ice storm destroyed one nesting flock and a forest fire destroyed another. Thus the supply was made less and the price higher without easing the market demand. The sawtimber was not destroyed by lumbering alone. Fire and clearing for agriculture reduced standing sawtimber without supplying any lumber demand.

The harp seal's population dynamics provides a *temporary*

resistance to the destruction motive. Harvesting of pups heavy enough to reduce total population just below the natural maximum serves to decrease the natural death rate and increase the birth rate. So the sustained-yield harvest had a wide margin for error. This explains the tendency to stable price and catch over so long a period. However, it must not be assumed that sustained-yield harvest of a living resource, even when combined with favorable population dynamics, is a foolproof arrangement. It so happens that a species' long-term viability depends upon its adaptability to change, and this adaptability is dependent upon the hidden supply of *recessive* genes spread thinly through a population. These recessive genes—unused and even burdensome in normal circumstances—become the salvation of a species when changing circumstances are inimical to the parent stock. So, commercial cropping of a living natural resource, even if the cropping causes no further decline in population, can result in extinction of a species if its adaptability is weak because of a paucity of recessive genes and some unfavorable change occurs in the species' environment. This genetic problem explains why it is not necessary for the commercial market to generate a price high enough to cover the uneconomical cost of tracking down the very last survivor: there is some critical population minimum for each species at any particular time and place. The commercial market *does not know what this critical minimum is* even if it cared.

Over the years, there have been claims and rumors that the American government encouraged the annihilation of the bison. The story is that the army decided that exterminating the bison would also starve the Indians: double genocide, so to speak. There seems to be some ugly evidence, but this is a question for historians to settle. So far as the economics of destruction is concerned, the "motive" has no need of such outside help. Actually, the economics of the bison was such that the *female* of the species was the more desired commodity: the meat brought a higher price and the hide was easier to skin off. The preferential killing of females made the population decline, and the rise in price, all the more precipitous. Some price data are available for the final decade of the industry. These are shown in Table 5-1, which also illustrates the method used to derive the indexes of real prices shown in Table 5-2. In Column A of Table 5-1 are the average wholesale unit prices for buffalo robes. These are derived mainly from raw data from a historical memorandum of purchases by J. and A. Buskowitz of New York and Chicago (see page 461 of *The North American Buffalo* by F. G. Roe, University of Toronto Press, 1951). In Column B are wholesale price indexes from *Historical Statistics of the United States*. In Column C are the real (deflated) prices for robes, calculated by dividing the current price by the wholesale price index. In Column D are the indexes of real prices for buffalo robes, with the earliest year shown (1872) set at 100. Thus the subsequent, irresistible, rise in price is shown clearly. For example in 1882, the last year of wholesale slaughter, the *real* price for robes was 640% higher than it was in 1872.

Table 5-1

WHOLESALE PRICES OF BUFFALO ROBES

Year	(A) Current Price	(B) Index of All Wholesale Prices	(C) Real Prices	(D) Index of Real Price
1872	$1.25	136	$ .92	100
1875	1.15	118	.98	106
1876	1.25	110	1.14	124
1877	3.81	106	3.60	390
1878	3.65	91	4.04	440
1879	3.86	90	4.20	465
1880	5.05	100	5.05	550
1881	6.50	103	6.30	685
1882	7.35	108	6.80	740

This *real price,* shown in Column C and, more clearly, as an index number in Column D, is a very important parameter in the resource destruction motive. If the real price, for any commodity uniquely nature's, is rising, it is presumptive evidence that the resource destruction motive is at work. Since trading in any commodity cannot take place without a *price,* then this parameter *must* have a determinate value. So the researcher has only, somehow, to ferret it out. This is not always the case for, say, the basic supply or the effectiveness of industrial methods. No one currently knows how much ore or petroleum remains below the surface or how many fish remain in the sea. Nor can we know for sure if or when current rates and methods of harvest will totally exhaust these resources. But if the real price is found to be rising, then we can be almost certain that the tendency is *toward that end.*

Now, the real price for lumber has been rising since 1875—and of our original stock of sawtimber we have only 10% left. The real price for iron ore has been rising since 1920; for petroleum since 1930; and for copper since 1932. Among the fishes, the real price for menhaden has been rising since 1926. The real price for haddock increased 100% from 1960 to 1970. The rising real prices *predict* that each is on its way toward exhaustion. But when, and how, will we come to *know* that this is true so that we will come to their rescue?

In the text of this chapter, current dollar prices were given in the examples simply to avoid being unnecessarily technical. In Table 5-2 the constant dollar, or real, prices are shown for some of the commodities that figured in the examples. They are expressed in index numbers similar to those in Column D of Table 5-1 and as explained above; that is, the earliest price depicted is set at 100 so that the subsequent rise is readily seen.

Table 5-2

Indexes of Real Price, Natural Resource Commodities

Year	(A) Passenger Pigeons	(B) Lumber	(C) Horse Meat	(D) Harp Seals
c.1800	100	—	—	—
c.1850	600	—	—	—
c.1875	2,200	100	—	—
c.1885	4,000	124	—	—
1900	Extinct	142	—	—
1920	—	236	—	—
1930	—	228	—	—
1940	—	300	—	—
1945	—	335	100	—
1950	—	480	128	100
1955	—	490	180	126
1960	—	430	—	195
1965	—	440	—	500
1970	—	455	—	—
1973	—	590	—	—

Specifications and Sources:

Column A: On New York market. A W. Schorger, *The Passenger Pigeon* (Madison, Wisconsin, 1955).

Column B: At the mill. Potter and Christy *Trends in Natural Resource Commodities* (except for 1965-73).

Column C: Boned and frozen, as received at cannery. Furnished by manufacturer.

Column D: Average value. Economics Intelligence Branch, Canadian Department of Fisheries, Ottawa.

6

URGENT BUSINESS

> The expanding economy, the necessity for which has become an Article of Economic Faith, has in hard fact been a contracting economy since it developed at the expense of such irreplaceable capital goods as soils and minerals and such theoretically renewable resources as water, forests, grasslands and wildlife.
>
> WILLIAM VOGT
> *Road to Survival*

Lately, throughout our land, growing numbers of Americans are becoming increasingly aware that some of America's natural resources are becoming alarmingly scarce. Only a small minority of voters are familiar with the seriousness of the situation, just yet. Indeed, if the majority knew the facts, we would see a concerted drive by democratic process for conservation of natural resources by some means or other. Actually, however, we are consuming our resource capital at a faster rate than ever before. This increasing rate of consumption is aggravating a situation that is already bad. As it gets worse and worse, it will be noticed more and more especially as shortages develop.

In the normal course of events, then, the problem of conservation will be faced sometime in the future. This would be heartening, of course, except that the problem *should* have been solved sometime in the past. You see, somewhere along the road to resource poverty we are rushing down there is, or was, a point of ruin: a point beyond which our material well-being will decline irreversibly. It would be useless, here, to speculate about the location of this point, in time or in extent of depletion. But it is obvious that the continued depletion of natural resources must result, eventually, in economic bankruptcy and social dis-

111

integration. So, it is of utmost urgency that we halt that process at the earliest possible time.

It is important to observe that our nation reached the current state of resource scarcity by an unusual, perhaps unique, procedure. In the past, societies have become resource-poor mainly through natural processes such as changes in climate or long occupancy, or by biological ones such as overpopulation. While these usual methods of impoverishment produce economic effects, the causative forces themselves can not be controlled by simple economic reforms. But no such intractable forces have impoverished America. Ours is a new country with beneficent climate, not yet impoverished by overpopulation. Our intention is to bankrupt ourselves by an economic process—the resource destruction motive—before time, the weather, or Malthusian multiplication get the chance. Unlike the changes in climate or the malignant reproduction of mankind, the resource destruction motive is not insuperable. One of the key parts of this complex incentive to destroy resources is a purely economic force. So, it is subject to control by social action.

We have seen that the human impulse on which this motive is founded is man's affinity for money. So, if there were no money-lust in men there would be no resource destruction motive. But this observation isn't very helpful. Indeed men also love the glories of nature, although this doesn't save them from destruction if destruction is the more profitable course. It is not unusual for a man whose riches came from lumbering to object to the cutting of trees along his street in order to widen the pavement. And a woman who flaunts a leopard coat might disapprove of her husband shooting rabbits. These are inconsistencies we see about us every day. Nothing much can be done about them.

In the absence of modern industrialism the resource destruction motive would not be a powerful force. The American Indians could not have killed all the bison and passenger pigeons, nor consumed all the high-grade iron ore in the Mesabi River range. We regret now that those terrible things were done, but those who were paid to do them were concerned only with devising more profitable and effective industrial methods to get the things to market. They felt no remorse. In any event, modern industrialism is a major part of our society. Nothing much can be done about that either.

Given these two forces only—industrialism and the profit incentive—there still would be no strong motive to destroy resources. Logically it would pay to cut trees no faster than they grow, for then the profit, and the industry, would go on forever. And send pigeons, furs, and fish to market only as fast as they reproduced. Ores and petroleum logically would be doled out—husbanded—so that the industry and income would continue over long periods. Reason and true self-interest would dictate arrangements such as these. But the laws of the market overcome reason and true self-interest. If trees are cut faster than they grow, they become scarcer and the price goes higher. And when the price goes higher most humans can't resist the increased reward. So, more trees are cut for the market, making trees scarcer and the prices higher still.

Of course, it is very doubtful whether we could alter the economic laws that apply in the marketplace—even if we wanted to. But, as you will see, that's not the idea at all. The fact is that the commercial market is a handy piece of economic machinery and, except for its part in the resource destruction motive, it works advantageously. Nowadays, the majority of things sold in the commercial market are the products of industry: light bulbs, bricks, bicycles, bathtubs and such-like useful articles. Modern industry can produce these things in greater or less supply as the occasion may demand: new machines can be added or existing ones shut down; manpower can be added or taken away, or diverted from the production of one product to another; new plants can be built or existing ones shut down. Really, no one doubts the ability of modern industry to flood the country with light bulbs, for example, or to stop their production altogether. And modern agriculture is not much less flexible than industry—although more time is required to effect a change: within a year wheat production could be greatly increased and corn production curtailed. The possibility of flooding the market with wheat, or producing none at all, is readily recognized. Ob-

viously there must be some economic facility for regulating these
things.

Along with the growth of industrialism, beginning early in
the nineteenth century, there evolved a price system that tends
effectively to regulate the production of industrial commodities.
It operates in such a manner that production varies *directly*
with prices. That is, when prices rise, production follows suit,
and vice versa. This is quite different from the price system
known as the "law of supply and demand." But it provides very
nicely for changes in demand. For example, if consumers want
more automobiles and fewer surreys with fringed tops, this
change in demand is sent to the producers through the commercial market by higher price bids for automobiles and lower
bids for surreys. Industry responds to these price changes by
increasing automobile production and decreasing the output of
surreys. This industrial price system actually gears the flexibility
of modern industry with the changing demands of the consumer.
In general then, prices and industrial production tend to rise and
fall together, that is, "in phase."

This industrial price system developed in an economic community which already had a natural price system in operation.
This latter—"the law of supply and demand"—operates on price
so that it tends to vary *inversely* with supply. When supply goes
up the price goes down and vice versa. This older natural price
system continues to function along with the industrial price
system, interacting with it in complex ways.

For industrial commodities, the industrial price system is
dominant. But the natural price system exerts its influence in a
moderating way tending to restrain price fluctuations. Should
the price for light bulbs rise, production will quickly rise. But
then, with the supply increased, the old law says the price should
fall. So there is a contest of forces, with the result that the price-
rise slows or halts. Then the newer law says that the production
rate should level off: stability is restored at the higher level.
Note that there is no suggestion here that increased industrial
production will cause industrial prices to *fall*. Under the dominant influence of the industrial price system, production rates

would rarely go so high as to cause prices to fall. Even so, and despite numerous defects in the industrial organization, it is clear that the two price systems work better than would either alone.

For modern agriculture, the two systems do not work so smoothly, but still the two are better than one. For agricultural commodities the natural price system is dominant in the short run. A crop failure will cause the price to rise; a bumper crop will cause a fall. The farmer lacks the precise short-term control enjoyed by industry. A rising price for light bulbs will quickly stimulate industry to increase production. But rising egg prices won't stimulate a molting hen. Thus the short-term movements of supply and price for agricultural products are "out of phase." But the farmer won't stay out of phase for long: if the long-term price movement for eggs and wheat is upward, long-term production will be upward too. The farmer tries to supply the market with what it wants, but it takes a little time. So the industrial price system is dominant only in the long run.

The farmers' problems have been discussed in an earlier chapter. There we learned that *aggregate* farm production tends always to increase whether the general price level is rising or falling. But how much of any year's aggregate should be corn and how much should be wheat? That is the question answered by the two price systems. Being dominant in the short run, the natural price system will penalize the farmer for raising too much of any product not in growing demand. On the other hand it will partly compensate his loss in the event of a poor crop by assigning a higher price for the reduced supply. And the secular change in demand and price will guide his longer-term plans, as it already has guided his change in emphasis, for example, from oats to soybeans and feed grains for meat animals.

The satisfactory operation of the two interacting price systems for both industry and agriculture occurs because both have control over how much of any product is to be produced. But nature cannot be so controlled. For those products uniquely nature's, the natural price system is dominant in the long run, to the end, and, sometimes, thereafter. But the industrial price system is operating, too, motivating industry to get the goods to market regardless of the ultimate consequences.

In the general case, the desired natural commodity is relatively accessible to industry. A good example would be our forests. The trees are both visible and immobile. So, the resource destruction motive operates on the commodity sawtimber in what may be called the typical manner. The industrial price system is dominant in the short run: a rise in price stimulates industry at once to increase cutting, and a fall in price immediately depresses cutting. These short-term fluctuations are "in phase," as would be the case for industrial products. But since cutting habitually exceeds the rate of sawtimber growth, the basic supply is getting scarcer in the long run, and the long-term price trend is upward—in accordance with the natural price system.

It is possible for industry to respond to a short-term price-rise by increasing cutting through greater effort and the use of more effective industrial methods. But this increased cutting further reduces the basic supply, and the increased rate of cutting cannot be sustained. The next short-term price-rise finds the industry less able to supply the market, so the price rises further than in the preceding cycle. The new rise in price calls forth greater effort to supply the market—which, of course, makes the situation all the worse for the next cycle. The rising prices cause the basic supply to be reduced; the reduction in basic supply causes a further rise in price. This process has been going on so relentlessly that in less than 50 years (1910-1956) the price of lumber increased over 750% in current dollars; over 300% in constant dollars. Despite this increased money reward, the lumber industry produced 14% less lumber in 1956 than in 1910. In the next 15 years, to 1971, real price rose by 33%, but production fell more than 3%.

Unlike forests, some resources are much less accessible and industry lacks good control of the short-run harvest. An example would be ocean fish. Fish move and they are hard to see. Thus the catch depends, in part, on luck. If the industry makes a lucky catch the price will fall; a poor catch and the price will rise. The natural price system is dominant in the short run, and the movements of price and supply will be out of phase, as for agricultural products. But if the fish are getting scarcer so that lucky catches are smaller and less frequent, the long-term price will rise. So greater catching effort will be employed, which will make fish scarcer yet.

Whether the process is typical (e.g., sawtimber), or atypical (e.g., fish), the end result of the operation of the resource destructive motive is the same for every commodity that cannot be, or is not, produced by commercial means, either industrial or agricultural. The same economic laws that operate satisfactorily for commercial items have the opposite effect on natural commodities. The natural price system says, "If a commodity becomes scarcer, the price shall rise"; the industrial price system adds, "If the price rises, more of the commodity must be sent to market." This synergism tends to continue until the resource is exhausted.

This destructive economic force has now been operating on our natural resources for at least one hundred years. Worse yet, since both population and industrial activity increased fairly steadily over the period, our resource capital has been subject to an assault of relentlessly increasing severity. So, at any time during the past century the status and progress of the process would give cause for alarm and concern for the future to anyone who could view the overall results comprehensively.

The first comprehensive study, however, did not appear until the end of World War II. This was *America's Needs and Resources*, made by the Twentieth Century Fund. The findings were indeed alarming: reserves of high-grade iron ore and commercial grades of lead, zinc and copper ores were greatly depleted; sawtimber drain was 50% greater than growth, etc., etc. Unfortunately, the country's main response to this clear warning was the postwar boom, with the drain on resources soon exceeding the peak wartime rates.

So the Twentieth Century Fund made a second study, which was published in 1955. The findings: America was becoming increasingly dependent on imports of *foreign* resources, with the most critical scarcity problems being petroleum, copper, lead, zinc and the ferroalloy metals.[1]

Actually the main benefit of these two Twentieth Century Fund studies was to inform and alert those few who read them. As for the nation as a whole the rates of consumption (exhaustion) for most resources continued to increase, as did the rate of imports of those so depleted that we were no longer self-sufficient.

In the next decade a new study was made, financed by the Ford Foundation. This, *Resources in America's Future,*[2] was published in 1963, just ten years before the petroluem crunch that was to temporarily arouse the nation. This new study concluded that "supply limitations are more likely to be a barrier to meeting projected demand for forest products than for any other major category of resource materials."[3]

While the Ford Foundation study judged the forests to be the worst long-term problem, it did not overlook the growing scarcity of minerals. It used the growing import rates to illustrate that America had depleted many of our most necessary resources and was now dependent on foreign supplies. Tabulated below is their estimate of net imports expressed as the average percent of U.S. consumption for the years 1956-60.

It was shocking to note that by the late 1950s America was no longer self-sufficient in those once-abundant resources—wood, petroleum, iron ore—that had made America the greatest industrial society. However, the 1963 study did little more to spur the country to start remedial action than did the two Twentieth Century Fund reports that preceded it. On the contrary, after 1963 the nation went on a binge of economic expansion, space exploration and war that resulted in increased waste and destruction of resources, setting records for both.

At this point we must face up to a terrible question. Why, with the facts developed by these three studies plus the warnings

[1]America's Needs and Resources, 1955.
[2]By Landsbergh *et al.,* (Baltimore: Johns Hopkins Press, 1963).
[3]*Ibid.,* p. 46.

Commodity	Amounted Imported
Lumber	10%
Petroleum	18%
Copper	18%
Pulpwood	25%
Iron ore	28%
Zinc	58%
Lead	75%
Manganese	90%
Aluminum and Bauxite	95%

of dozens of other studies and books published since 1945, have we continued to plunge down the road to self-destruction? Our society is the most widely educated, with the best facilities for communication and dissemination of information. The pollution and waste associated with our ever-growing rate of consumption of resource capital is clearly—obscenely—visible to each of us. Very few are spared the sight of some local consequence: the spilled oil, the horrible scars of strip mines and clear-cut forest land visible from the air, the shocking mounds of solid waste, the ubiquitous hulks of rusting autos, the litter of discarded bottles and cans. We have a reasonably effective system for self-government to provide for common action when it is required. And yet we continue on the course toward self-inflicted impoverishment. Why?

If the answer lies within our genetic programming—as is suspected for the trait known as "discounting the future"—then, of course, our industrial society will decline spasmodically and our experiment in self-government will end during one of the spasms. However, if the answer is that the resource destruction motive is so powerful that no existing social force can stop it, then it is not nearly so hopeless. In other words, if the fault lies within us we are soon at the end, but if the fault is in the commercial market we can overcome it.

Surely the resource destruction motive is the most probable explanation for the practical failure of most of our past efforts at conservation. Also it explains the few successes.

The main and most hopeful effort at conservation to date

applied to American forests. The effort was based on (1) public ownership of some of the forest land and (2) forest management to be encouraged by a U.S. Forest Service. It began with an act of Congress in 1891 and was largely "in place" by the end of Theodore Roosevelt's term in 1908.

Now note this: an inventory of our timber resources made in 1909 showed an estimated stand of sawtimber of 2.8 trillion board feet; an estimate made in 1945 showed a total stand of 1.6 trillion. So, in the first 36 years of America's forest conservation the sawtimber resources of the nation were *depleted by 44%!* What caused the failure? The resource destruction motive, of course. About three-fourths of commercial forest land remained in private hands. So, cutting followed the price set by the commercial market: there were no restraints. As the forests were depleted the real prices for timber products rose, stimulating increased cutting effort and advancing technologies.

The National Forests, on the other hand, were subject to some restraints and as of 1970 contained over 50% of our remaining stand of sawtimber. There is no economic compulsion to overcut the National Forests, and the general management philosophy has been that of sustained-yield. However, lobbying by the private forest cutters is powerful, especially during times of rapidly rising prices for wood products. As a result, private practices such as clear-cutting (completely denuding large areas of forest land) are now used on our National Forests. During the Nixon years a strong attempt was made to further increase cutting because of rising prices, but the attempt was halted by the courts. There is an important lesson here: economic laws do not *always* prevail over statutory laws.

Among the few successful efforts at conservation the main one was the saving of our wild bird life from commercial extermination. Why it succeeded can be seen in the following quotation from Ludlow Griscom, writing as chairman of the Audubon Society in 1950:

By 1920 every North American bird was protected, the Federal Government had taken control of all migratory birds, any form of commercial use of native birds was illegal . . . the results have been most gratifying.[4]

What had been accomplished was this: the wild bird life of America was legally declared off limits for the profit incentive, the power of modern industry *and* the price laws of the market-place. This triple-barreled solution was no doubt made possible by the widespread public sympathy for such innocent and beautiful creatures as birds, especially after what had happened to so many species that had been taken to market.

Unfortunately, the resource destruction motive does not limit its deadly force to the pretty birds. It also destroys the standing forests, the fossil fuels, the mineral ores, and the unseen aquatic life. There is little spontaneous sympathy for a log or a lobster or a lump of ore. Besides, all these natural resources must be used to maintain our society; they can not be taken completely out of the market. For our society to endure, however, they must be conserved.

But the conservation movement has failed—stymied by the some economic force that destroys the resources. So economic reform is the most urgent business. The resource destruction motive must be curbed by effectual social reform. Then and only then can conservation become a viable national policy.

---

[4]*Birds of America* (New York: Macmillan, 1950), p. 23.

PART II

A
NEW
ECONOMY

7

A CURE FOR MONEY MADNESS

> Unemployment develops, that is to say, because people
> want the moon;—men cannot be employed when the ob-
> ject of desire (i.e., money) is something which cannot be
> produced and the demand for which cannot be readily
> choked off.
>
> JOHN MAYNARD KEYNES
> *The General Theory of Employment,*
> *Interest and Money* (P. 235)

On August 24 in the year 79, the Roman city Pompeii was
smothered with volcanic ash from violently erupting Mount
Vesuvius. Many of the inhabitants were trapped and buried with
their city. Centuries later, on April 18, 1748, explorers probing
the site of the ancient disaster uncovered a human skeleton. To
their delight—although they saw nothing of economic significance
in it—they found gold and silver coins near the bones of the
skeleton's hand. This ill-fated Pompeian must have been clutch-
ing the coins as he ran. It is even possible that he lost his race for
life because he stopped to get them. But, wherever he thought
he was going, his intentions, clearly, were to take his money with
him.

Since this man was in the midst of a volcanic eruption, we
know that he had no immediate purchase in mind. That is, he
certainly wasn't running to the nearest store. Further, we can
surmise that he had no definite plans for a specific future purchase. Even so, with his future rapidly coming to an end, he
sought the solace of money as insurance against the future. Some
behavior pattern, or reflex, impelled him to provide himself with
money for some vague eventuality. Now, a mode of financial
conduct that would have enabled this Pompeian, or encouraged

or conditioned him, to run for his life *without* money is the very thing that we are seeking. In other words, if this peculiar quality of money that makes such fools of men, and such a shambles of their economic affairs, can be nullified, then much progress will have been made toward the correction of one of the major faults of our economic system.

First, however, let's expose a false trail. The monetary shortfall and all its unpleasant results cannot be cured simply by forbidding the use of debt! True, the present accumulations of pecuniary riches by the few are made possible only by the indebtedness of the many. So, it may appear that the gullible debtors are the instigators of the monetary shortfall. But such a view fails to note that even without debt the monetary shortfall would plague us, for then the rich would accumulate *currency* to the point of stifling the economy; that is, the acquisitive will accumulate credit-money and collect the interest on it so long as the rest of us are foolish enough to go into debt. But if we fail to increase our debts, the acquisitive will accumulate currency-money. So you see it is the avarice of men, not their gullibility, that underlies our financial troubles.

Nor will we solve the problem by deploring these things. There must be some deeply felt needs for monetary savings on the one hand, and debt on the other; that is, there may be motives other than avarice, and weaknesses other than gullibility —or, perhaps, other forces back of them. Surely most people would not spend more than their incomes unless it seemed necessary. Nor would others struggle to accumulate fortunes unless there were some impelling need. Of course, there are a few who want riches for their own sake, or for the power brought by such riches. Others may seek the status of *rentiers* in order to indulge in the fulsome leisure made possible by receiving the interest on perpetual debt. For these few there is no defense. They are the lunatic fringe of economic society: the greedy, the tyrants, the parasites and wastrels. But it would be unseemly to say that ordinary thrift is financial lunacy. The desire for security, protection from the rigors of poverty, and insurance against possible misfortunes are motives we can understand and sympathize with.

Individuals, then, are naturally concerned about their own future security. Monetary savings, seemingly, can provide some insurance against many of the unpleasant things that might happen in the future. But the supply of legal currency is so limited compared with all the possible needs and misfortunes that can be imagined for the days ahead. This relatively inelastic amount of legal money has led, accidentally perhaps, to the use of credit-money as savings against life's uncertainties. We have seen that credit (debt) is much more expandable than the supply of currency. However, the expansion of debt has its limit, too. And when the expansion does come to an end serious economic difficulties ensue. Neither in theory nor in actual practice does the holding of debts provide a foolproof form of saving for future needs, or insurance against future troubles. Besides, just when you most need to collect on the debts you might discover: they cannot be repaid.

Nor is currency a good form of insurance. Primarily, currency is the legal medium of exchange: a convenience to use in conducting the day's business. To serve this basic role the quantity of it should remain fairly stable, growing only in step with the growth of population and standard of living. For this reason, control of the legal money supply is assigned exclusively to the government. But currency also can be used as a store of value; that is, it can be held indefinitely for possible future need. It is to this aspect of money that men have assigned some of the qualities of insurance: to be used for, or held against, possible future emergencies or a feared "rainy day." Let us assume for the moment that money actually could buy away all the unpleasant things that *could* happen. Even so, it should be obvious that it is impossible for the government to maintain a stable medium of exchange, and at the same time provide an ever-expanding supply to satisfy the limitless human craving for insurance against all possible future emergencies or future wants.

As can be seen, then, neither currency-money nor debt-money provides adequately for the reasonable need for security. However, there *is* a modern economic device—insurance—which *could* provide financial protection against future emergencies. At present, however, our foolish financial habits are carried over into the institutions that "sell" insurance. We find them acting merely as brokers for risk. They lend out the premium payments they receive in an attempt to sublet the responsibility for covering their clients' future claims. Here is one more effort to associate security with debt. Besides, we find that these institutions are interested primarily, not in making insurance, but in making "money." They, too, play the game of taking in more than they pay out. Then when, because of such money madness, a financial panic is brought upon us, the insurance companies are found to be just as insolvent[1] as the banking system and the rest of the economy. All are dependent on the same phantom foundation: debt. Many of the possible benefits of insurance are thereby lost just when they are needed most. So, the main purpose of the concept of insurance is defeated.

But this defeat—this failure—is the result of foolish financial habits that are not necessary. That is, it is not necessary to assign to money a dual role of medium of exchange *and* insurance. Nor is it necessary to assign to debt the quality of insurance. You see, we have an economic device—insurance—which does have the quality we are seeking. So, with debt out of use, and money in use solely as a medium of exchange, we can visualize expanded insurance coverage that would furnish all the security we can earn. We can visualize insurance so universal and so sound that it would ease disquietude as well as would money and debts, and provide a much sounder method of "buying away" those misfortunes that actually do develop. In truth, we already have economic concepts available that could do the job. It is really only our financial conduct that is in error.

Even as we set about planning the necessary reforms, we realize there is an obstacle: inertia. Our society seems very

---

[1]During the last depression considerable effort by the state governments, and the federal government through the RFC, was required to keep the insurance companies from collapsing. Many life insurance companies refused to pay the cash surrender values on their policies so they would have enough funds to pay off death benefits.

resistant to reform. But, as time goes by, the defects of our economy become more widely known. Also, eventually, there will occur some kind of a crunch: a depression, perhaps. Sooner or later, then, and for one good reason or another, we will find ourselves more than willing to make some changes. So, let us set down the changes that have to be made. And reserve for later judgment how practicable these necessary reforms will be.

A. We must eliminate the need for going into debt. (This would curtail the opportunity for making loans—accumulating, that is.)

B. We must greatly expand the scope of our insurance setup and put it on a sound basis.

C. We must devise some financial instrument to substitute for monetary savings. (This would eliminate the need for hoarding or lending.)

D. We must arrange to have all the income of all the people flow into two main channels: consumption and investment.

E. We must cast off the dead weight of existing debt. (This would eliminate the oppressive burden of interest.)

Now, it is possible to accomplish the first three—*A, B* and *C,* that is—merely by changing the rules under which insurance companies operate. This will be called the "insurance technique." With the insurance technique in operation, there will be little opportunity to lend (accumulate) because borrowing won't be necessary. Nor will there be a need to hoard. That will leave only two channels—consumption and investment—for money to flow into. But we humans have such a terrible affinity for money that it will be necessary also to socialize savings. This latter reform is necessary to insure that money income actually does flow into the two channels. Getting rid of existing debt will be relatively easy—except for the paperwork.

So, we have resolved the five perplexing things we must do into a three-part reform program that we could do: an insurance technique; the socialization of savings; and the elimination of existing debt.

PART I. THE INSURANCE TECHNIQUE

At present, insurance companies are licensed and regulated by the states. Actually, however, the right to regulate insurance companies legally belongs to the federal government.[2] It would be both legal and practicable, then, for the government to require that all insurance companies operate so that each company's net income, in excess of the claims, is used for investments that will be self-liquidating without charging interest. This is best explained by examples.

Suppose that an insurance company takes in $1,000,000 more in a month than it must pay out for expenses and claims. To invest this million, the company would, for example, build fifty $20,000 houses. These houses would be sold to individuals on a rental-applied-to-purchase-price basis. The rental-purchase price would be set at an amount that would return to the insurance company the cost of each house plus all expenses and a sales profit, but excluding interest. The ownership of each house would pass to the rent-purchaser after he had paid off the total price. As these rental-purchase payments return to the insurance company they would be used to pay claims, or, if claims are lacking, to build more houses. So, each insurance company would be getting income from two sources: premium payments, and rental-purchase payments. And the excess of this income over the claims that are paid would be continually reused for interest-free investments.

In like manner, the next $1,000,000 could be used to build a new school, or sewage treatment plant, for rental-purchase by a local government, with payments made each year or month out of tax receipts or service charges. The next million could be used to build a facility for rental-purchase by the federal government. And the next million to build a factory, an airliner, or machine tools, for rental-purchase by private corporations.

Note at this point that the insurance companies will be paying

---

[2]See U.S. v. Southeastern Underwriters Assn. 322US533 (1944).

out all they take in, getting back all they pay out, and, in the process, creating investment goods and selling them on a basis that *eliminates interest and the need for mortgage, public, or corporate debt.*

Now, for each dollar of premiums that a person paid in, there would be a dollar's worth of insurance policies issued to him. These policies could provide coverage for death benefits, sickness, accident, loss of any kind, bankruptcy, unemployment, retirement. In fact, insurance coverage can be provided to restore an individual's financial loss from practically any misfortune that can be imagined. And each dollar in premiums will be invested, recovered, reinvested—out and back—until it is needed to pay a claim. So, from the standpoint of the insurance company, each dollar will be invested or spent (by the person who had a loss and made a claim). A little thought will reveal that, from the standpoint of the people who are insured, the dollars flowing into the investment channels *are their savings*—ready to be paid to them when needed. That strange-seeming idea that investment and savings are identical should now become clear.

Before we go on to the next part of the problem, note that, as developed this far, the insurance technique provides for all reasonable need for financial security against misfortune. But there is nothing unorthodox in this! Ever since insurance was developed, there existed the possibility that the concept could be expanded to provide all the economic security that the economy could support. That this expansion did not come about was not the fault of our concept of insurance; it was the fault of our concept of *money*. Which brings us to the problem of a substitute for money-savings.

In the insurance technique, in addition to standard-type policies, there would be *insurance certificates*. These would be deliberately endowed with many of the qualities of monetary savings. For example, suppose that a saver (the insured) preferred to save for future *wants* instead of, or in addition to, saving for security (regular insurance). In this case, the insurance company would issue insurance *certificates* to the saver. And he could use these in any of the following ways:

1. The saver could spend his certificates to buy new capital or durable goods built to his specifications. Here can be seen the main difference between insurance policies and *certificates:* if the saver's income is put into insurance the insurance company will invest it as it sees fit; if the saver puts his savings into *certificates,* then he may invest his savings as *he* sees fit.

2. If the saver found an existing asset—a house or business establishment, for example—that was for sale, he could give up his certificate to the seller. The insurance company would transfer certificates in the amount of the sale price from the buyer to the seller.

3. The saver could buy stocks in the stock market in the same way. Or a corporation could sell stock to savers in exchange for their certificates. Then the corporation would "spend" them in, for the new plant or machinery built to their specifications.

4. The owner of certificates—whether the original owner, or a new one—could convert the certificates into insurance policies.

5. The saver of certificates could donate them to a church, or university, or research foundation, or charity.

6. The saver could hoard certificates to his heart's content. Of course, while he is hoarding the certificates, his savings in an amount equal to the certificates will have been invested by the insurance companies.

7. The saver of certificates could redeem them for a cash refund on a basis that will be described under the next part—the socialization of savings.

This completes the basic outline of the insurance technique. Greatly expanded insurance will provide for financial protection against misfortune. Insurance certificates—salvable, spendable, negotiable, investable, convertible, donatable, hoardable, and redeemable—will take the place of monetary savings. If you are the saver of insurance and certificates, they will be registered in your name at your insurance company. Then if you get caught in a volcanic eruption, run. Your savings are safe. And your loss is insured.

PART II. THE SOCIALIZATION OF SAVINGS

Read the Constitution of the United States and you will find that the federal government is assigned the exclusive right *to coin the money and regulate the value thereof*. The right of coinage obviously carries with it the right of controlling the *aggregate* supply of money. But to control the value thereof—the purchasing power of money, that is—requires much more than merely the control of aggregate supply. To insure a stable economy and prevent inflation or deflation (changes in the value of money), it is necessary to prevent the *maldistribution* of money, and the *misuse* of money. The Constitution not only assigns the government the right to do this, but implies the duty of doing it.

As we all know, the government has a firmly established system for collecting income taxes. It would be both practicable and constitutional, then, for the government to assess and collect the insurance premiums (savings) of all the people.[3] This would assure that these savings actually would flow into the investment channel of the insurance technique. The rates of saving could be set high enough so that "take-home" income would be used mainly for consumption. This idea is best explained by example. In the table are listed, for illustration, representative amounts of income tax, take-home cash, and insurance (savings) assessments as they might apply to individual incomes ranging from $5,000 to $5,000,000 a year.

You should examine the table as each column is explained. Column 1, total income, means exactly that. It is the individual's annual total of wages, salary, profits, dividends, long-and short-term capital gains, gifts, windfalls, inheritance—everything. At present, different types of income are taxed differently. But this is largely sheer favoritism—for the benefit of the rich. Did you

[3]Currently, about 15% of the premiums paid by the insured is siphoned off just to pay the insurance "salesmen." Since this sales cost will be eliminated it will more than compensate for the loss of interest receipts.

(1)	(2)	(3)	(4)
		Take-Home Pay	Insurance Assessment
Individual's Total Income	Income Tax	(Cash for Spending)	(Savings-Investment)
$ 5,000	$ 250	$ 4,000	$ 750
10,000	1,000	6,800	2,200
20,000	2,800	11,200	6,000
50,000	10,000	19,000	21,000
100,000	25,000	25,000	50,000
500,000	150,000	50,000	300,000
1,000,000	300,000	75,000	625,000
5,000,000	1,500,000	150,000	3,350,000

ever wonder why wages and salaries were taxed more heavily than stock market profits? All such inequities will be excluded from the insurance technique.

Column 2, income tax, you will note, is not nearly so steeply progressive as existing rates. Why? Because it will be based on only two things: the ability to pay, and the government's need for income. At present, our steep tax rates are based also on a third thing: the need to correct the maldistribution of income. This latter idea derives from Keynes's General Theory. It is theoretically sound but it has not proved workable. In England, the tax rates are partially effective in leveling incomes. But the idea doesn't work so well for us. And it works even worse in France and Italy. So, under the insurance technique, income tax rates will reach a maximum of about 30% on million-dollar incomes. And when the government's need for ballistic missiles and surplus farm products becomes less, the tax rates can be reduced—without worrying about the maldistribution of income. That will be taken care of by other means.

In Column 3 is the take-home pay. This is based on only one thing: the amount that might usefully be spent for consumption without squandering or hoarding. The suggested rates in the table are only tentative. In actual practice these should be determined by scientific studies of consumption (spending) habits.

The problem will be to set the amount that will keep hoarding or extravagance to a minimum, and yet permit each person to share (equitably, but not equally) the current output of goods and services.

Column 4, of course, is the important one. This amount of insurance assessment (savings) is the difference between a person's total year's income from all sources and the amount of it that he and his government spend for consumption. Note that total income minus spending equals saving (investment). This insurance (savings) assessment will be collected from each person through the income tax collection system. Then, in the name of the person from whom it is collected, it will be turned over to the insurance company of his choice. The company will issue to the saver the policies and certificates that he chooses. And the savings will flow into the investment channel of the insurance technique.

So, we have completed the cycle. The money goes round and round, out and back, without getting stuck, and there are some pleasant extra advantages that could be built in, too. For example, the government could give up the veteran's insurance and unemployment insurance business. These would be handled by the insurance companies. Unions could do likewise with their welfare fund business. Corporations could transfer their retirement and unemployment payment plans directly to the insurance companies. "Fringe" benefits, for example, could be added directly to the employee's insurance fund.

And that novel instrument, the insurance certificate, could be endowed with liquidity by making it fully redeemable in cash. This could be done providing that the cash refund from the certificates is treated just like all other income; that is, the amount of certificates redeemed in cash would constitute cash income and would be fully subject to income tax and insurance assessments. Suppose, for example, that the millionaire (see the $1,000,000 income in the table) elected to hold his $625,000 savings divided between $125,000 in insurance policies (for security) and $500,000 in certificates (for liquidity). The certificates could be used in any of the ways listed previously. But so long as the millionaire was making his million or more every year, he could gain little extra take-home income by turning the certificates in for cash. However, if the million had been made on a one-shot basis—for example, a best-selling book, a prize fight, or an invention, never to be repeated—it would be impossible for him ever to go broke. By cashing in certificates at $100,000 a year he would have a $25,000 take-home cash income for five years, at which time he will have amassed $250,000 in new certificates (that is, each year the $100,000 income resulting from cashing in the certificates will be assessed $25,000 for taxes and $50,000 for new insurance certificates). Now he can cash in at the rate of $50,000 a year for five years. This will give him $19,000 a year take-home income and leave him $105,000 in savings. Eventually, of course, his cash income must be further reduced, but however prodigal he may be he could never become destitute.

But there still remains a fly in the ointment. Although the insurance certificates provide both a store-of-value and liquidity, they do not eliminate these same qualities in money. In other words, insurance certificates are salvable and hoardable, *but so is money.* So, the take-home cash (Column 3) would be subject to hoarding. And there seems little that we can do about it except to offer some reward for not hoarding. Our difficulty is this: the insurance technique eliminates the need for debt and the ever-growing burden of interest. But it does not eliminate entirely the need for interest, nor the rate of interest.

Now, we have taken a dim view of the absurdity of paying a reward to some for not having hoarded forty times as much money as there is. And we hold a similar view of the banker's hocus-pocus system of accepting deposits of ten times as much money as there is and lending it all out to people who quickly get rid of it. So, let us simply require the banking system to maintain cash reserves of 50%. Then each dollar that found its way into the banking system could be lent out just once. Interest would be paid on savings accounts as at present, thus providing a reward for not hoarding. And the banking system would make loans on which interest would be charged. But, in amount, these loans could never exceed the amount of the currency supply, because of the 50% reserve that the banks would be required to maintain.

At this point it is worth noting that we have assembled some strong deterrents against the hoarding of money. Insurance policies being so sound and so widely held, would do much to ease disquietude. Insurance certificates would provide for liquidity and hoarding—in fact were devised with that in mind. Banks would be so sound, because they have 50% reserves, that those who refrain from spending all their take-home pay need not fear to deposit it. Most important, perhaps, the take-home pay itself would not be so large that hoarding could reach very large proportions.

Now, there is one more exceedingly important economic benefit that could be derived from the insurance technique. Since the insurance companies will be habitually carrying on large investment activities, it would be practicable for them to change the emphasis and tempo in such a way as to keep prices stable. This would be guided by the central monetary authority. For example, let us say that prices are rising for textiles and appliances, tending to raise the whole price index. So, the investment (construction) rate for housing, highways, etc., could be slowed (by working, say, thirty-five hours per week), and investments in textile and light industry speeded up. The net effect would be to reduce effective demand for all products while increasing the capacity to supply those in high demand. A falling price index would be treated conversely.

With the insurance technique, the central monetary authority (federal government, that is) would, at last, have sufficient control to regulate the value of money as required by the Constitution. Demand and purchasing power could be reduced (to stop inflation, for example) simply by slowing down the investment tempo. If the insurance companies merely delayed the start of new investments, funds from premium and rental receipts would soon build up in their hands. Here they would be held out of circulation in the required amount and for the required time. Thus the money supply and effective demand (enhanced by the investment multiplier) could be swayed together to bear against a trend toward inflation or, conversely, against deflation.

Such powerful and precise control over the effective money supply would be unprecedented. So, its full potentialities would have to be determined by experience. Indeed, it might turn out that central federal control could be limited to regulating the amount of funds to be held sterile and the time they are to be held. Thus, the type of investments could continue as a matter for private decision free from governmental interference.

Indeed, any good attempt to stabilize prices would be reinforced by undermining some nasty current practices. Nowadays, if people expect prices to fall—or note that they are falling—they are prone to hold back from spending. You see, they expect that by holding their money they will get more for it later. It works, too. That is, this withholding of effective demand makes prices all the weaker. Conversely, if people see that prices are rising they soon realize that their money is losing its value. So, they spend it quickly, which of course, makes the price inflation all the worse. Even approximate price stability would greatly weaken the motives for these attacks of speculative money madness. Under the insurance technique we might find that price stability can be achieved practicably and with relative ease.

PART III. THE ELIMINATION OF EXISTING DEBT

You might think it a harebrained idea to tear up three trillion dollars in bonds, mortgages and bank loans (i.e., deposits). And yet existing debt is worth only the paper it is printed on. So, the only loss in tearing it up would be the paper. True, these debts are legal promises to pay. But the promises can't be kept, no matter how hard those who promised make the attempt.

In ancient times this was perceived. In classical Greece, after the introduction of coined money, indebtedness soon became troublesome and, finally, intolerable. So, in 594 B.C. under Solon's *Seisachtheia* debts were cancelled. The ancient Hebrews set aside one year every fifty as a Jubilee: debts were forgiven and bondmen set free. A colleague of Keynes, Joan Robinson, pointed

out how well a Jubilee might work in a modern capitalist economy: debts would be forgiven and a fresh start could be made.
It is doubtful whether a fresh start in the same direction would
ever amount to very much. But the idea would certainly work
well with the insurance technique: only one Jubilee would be
needed!

Even so, a Jubilee would be a drastic operation and could be
very painful. For example, cancelling all debts would wipe out
most of the assets (paper assets, of course) of insurance companies and banks. This might be practical if a new great depression progressed to the point that the insurance companies
and the banking system actually collapsed. In theory they could
collapse quite easily—when it became obvious that their assets
(our debts) are worthless because our debts cannot be repaid.

However, it is not likely that such total collapse would be
permitted by the government. Inflation (by expansion of the
money supply) is a fairly practical palliative. As a depression
deepens, the need for more money becomes so acute that currency inflation automatically becomes the "cure." As more and
more people face delinquency, bankruptcy and dispossession because of the lack of money to pay their debts, the demand for
more money (inflation) becomes imperative. In fact, whenever,
and wherever, the burden of debt becomes too heavy, the forces
toward devaluation and inflation set in. The French franc, for
example, was worth thirty cents around the time of World War
I. By 1959, it was worth only about two-tenths of one cent. On
the average, it took 450 francs in 1959 to buy what one franc
would have bought in 1913. On August 10, 1969, the franc was
devalued for the thirteenth time in forty-one years. But despite
this "easy" cure the French are still in debt. And their economy
seems always near the point of collapse.

We shall find the German method of inflation much more
interesting. After World War I, Germany was intolerably bur-
dened by debt. At that time, par for the German mark was about
five to the dollar. That is, one dollar would pay off debts of five
marks. Late in 1922 the devaluation was started and by January
1923 a dollar would pay off debts of 7,260 marks. This was only

the beginning. By July 1923 a dollar would pay off a million marks of debt. By November 1923 it was *four billion.* In a way, it was easy. A German could export a dozen hankies and get enough money to pay off all his debts, including his mortgage. In fact, this fast type of inflation is the one way that aggregate debts can be paid off. Then (November 1923) the Germans created a new mark worth one billion of the old ones. So, they were back where the thing started—except that most of the old debt was gone.

Very clever. But it had its painful aspects. Pensions, savings, insurance, educational and research endowments were gone, too. But the German economy survived the "cure." And it was all over in about a year. This brings us to an interesting point: it practically was a Jubilee. You see, if inflation is carried out fast enough it approaches a Jubilee. From the French experience we can see that, if it isn't done fast enough, it cures nothing. Their system of inflation may be likened to spending forty years trying to cut off an infected finger. The Germans got all set up and sawed it off. But it's probably best to take it off in one quick whack, and cry "Jubilee."

So, the idea of tearing up the debt isn't so harebrained after all. It is, in fact, both logical and ethical. It is a principle of law that sons are not liable for their fathers' debts. So, since the fathers cannot pay the debt, why not tear it up? Well, it would be revolutionary; it would have painful aspects; and such things seldom work out to be so easy as they look.

Suppose, then, that we haven't the stomach for a "Jubilee," but we insist on something that isn't just temporary like the easy cure by inflation. Some other method, then, must be devised. An attempt will be made here to outline a practicable alternative: that is, a plan to change this three-trillion-dollar debt into non-debt form. It is assumed, of course, that the insurance technique has been put in operation.

Below is an itemized tabulation of the net debt outstanding as of January 1, 1975. In the text following the table, each item will be examined for a practical way to convert it into non-interest-bearing form compatible with the insurance technique:

Item	Category	Net Debt*
1.	Federal government and federal agencies	$ 437 billion
2.	State and local government	206 "
3.	Corporate long-term	550 "
4.	Corporate short-term	704 "
5.	Mortgage and farm debt	607 "
6.	Consumer, commercial, financial (individual non-mortgage)	273 "
	Total	$2,777 billion

Source: Table 2, p. 10, *Survey of Current Business*, July 1975.

Item 1, federal debt. Under the then prevailing circumstances of constantly increasing federal debt, when old bonds fell due, the government simply issued new ones to take their place. The government, however, kept up the interest payments, using tax receipts. It thereby transferred the fruits of labor from one group to another. By these dubious acts, the United States maintained its reputation as the safest credit risk in the country: a very useful myth to help bolster a papier-mâché economy.

The legal basis for the transformation of this debt to non-debt form will be the constitutional[4] obligation to regulate the value of money, and a step toward this end is the virtual elimination of interest-bearing debt. This will clear the way for redeeming the *principal* amount of the public debt. Redemption can be achieved by making, say, twenty annual payments of 5% of the face value of the bonds. Thus, the entire principal would be repaid. The annual cost in tax money would be about equal to current annual interest expense. Nothing intolerable in that. Nor

---

[4]The Constitution grants to Congress the authority to make all laws "necessary and proper" for carrying into execution the constitutional powers of the federal government. In this case, it is the problem of regulating the value of money through the operation of the insurance technique. The elimination of existing debt is one of the acts required *toward that end*. In Maryland vs. McCulloch, Chief Justice Marshall ruled that if the "end be legitimate" and within the scope of the Constitution, then all means "which are plainly adopted to that end" are constitutional.

need we be anguished because the burden falls on the sons of those who fell into the trap of debt. Given the old order of things, there was no other way. At least the sons will have the stock of capital and wealth of technology as a bequest from those who labored before them.

Item 2, state and local debt, can be divided into two distinct parts. One part is actually secured by self-liquidating assets such as toll roads and other utilities. The debt so secured could be redeemed through the insurance technique. The insurance companies would buy the bonds at face value with insurance policies or certificates. The governments would make rental-purchase payments out of tolls or service charges. The remainder of state and local debt would be redeemed by annual payments out of tax revenues as described for Item 1 above.

Item 3 is largely corporate bonded debt. This is quite easy to redeem. The individual corporations will simply issue to the bond holders a first preference stock paying dividends at a rate equal to the interest rate of the bonds. Indeed, it would have been much better to have used preferred stock in the first place, because it would have greatly reduced the danger of bankruptcy.

Item 4, corporate short-term debt, is a difficult category to deal with. This debt is usually reduced during the early phases of a credit contraction (incipient depression). And some is cancelled by bankruptcies as the depression worsens. No doubt before the insurance technique reform actually could be adopted, the depression would have progressed to a point where much of this short-term debt no longer existed on the books. Of what's left, that portion secured by working capital and inventories can be assumed by the new banking system. The portion secured by plant and equipment could be assumed by the insurance companies and recovered on a rental-applied-to-purchase-price basis.

Item 5, mortgage and farm debt, strange as it may seem, could be a boon to the insurance technique because it would help to start it off on a volume basis. These mortgages could be taken over by the insurance companies. Then, the mortgagees could pay off the unpaid balance on a rental basis that would include all expenses but without interest. This would give the present tenants (including many farmers) an excellent chance to become owners of the properties they occupy. Also it would provide the insurance companies with assets and an income fund (from the rental payments) to enable them to keep existing insurance in force and pay claims that arise. If an individual held a mortgage he could turn it into an insurance company and get policies or certificates equal to the unpaid balance of the mortgage. Savings and loan associations could be merged into the insurance companies. Mortgages held by banks could be transferred to the insurance companies in exchange for insurance certificates, which in turn could be used to pay off depositors. Fortunately, insurance companies already hold quite a chunk of these mortgages.

Item 6. About 15% of the debt under this item is commercial borrowing mainly from banks, where it could remain, without conversion, as an acceptable interest-bearing form of bank credit to cover the interest on savings accounts. Another 15% is financial borrowing secured by stocks, bonds and insurance reserves; that portion held by banks could remain as is, that held by insurance companies could be liquidated by cancelling the indentured amount of the borrowers' insurance. The remaining 60% of Item 6 is consumer credit secured only by partly consumed goods. This could be liquidated as it is repaid on the original installment schedule and replaced by a new system wherein banks extend interest-bearing installment credit to consumers who make 50% down payments.

※　※　※

This, then, is an outline of a mode of financial conduct—the insurance technique—that could cure the monetary shortfall. A desirable form of true savings—insurance—is offered as an outlet for thrift. An equal value of investments—physical assets—is offered for rental-purchase by those who will pay to use them. The insurance will satisfy all reasonable motives for saving in an economically sound manner. The investment will provide durable assets (of the type now acquired mostly with debt) on a rental-purchase and self-liquidating basis. This basis will be so much more favorable to the buyers than the existing debt-interest basis that the instruments known as bonds and mortgages will fall into disuse.

With the introduction of this financial technique, which eliminates the need for further debt, the burden of past debts can be *cast off once and for all.* With the disappearance of existing debt a most amazing set of simultaneous events will necessarily take place:

1. The pecuniary poor—i.e., those who owe more than they have—will be absolved.

2. The functionless *rentiers* will lose that status, and their interest-paying "slaves" will be set free.

3. Negative savings (debt) suddenly will become zero, and positive savings, therefore, will equal investment.

4. With the identity of savings and investment established, and with lending out of use because no one needs to borrow, the nation's aggregate income will be directed almost solely into consumption and investment (i.e., saving). Production, therefore, will create its own demand. That is, each man's income—no matter how large or how small it is—will be spent either for consumption, or for investments that will provide for future consumption.

This new arrangement, called the "insurance technique" is really only a change in the way we conduct our financial affairs. It is not revolutionary, but the rewards—both social and economic —to be gained by eliminating debt and the monetary shortfall are little short of astounding. Great depressions will be eliminated because all production will create an equal demand and an equal amount of purchasing power. All that the American economy can produce can then be purchased without debt. Even so, every person will be able to save all he can afford to save.

Of course, there will still be the rich and, in a relative way, the poor. But none will be poor in the sense that he owes more than he has. And none will be enslaved under the bonds of interest on perpetual debt. Nor will the rich be rich in the sense that they have great accumulations of monetary riches. Rather the rich will be rich in security. Of course, everyone will have some security and some share of the economic things produced. But the more successful will have the larger share of both.

8

THE PREREQUISITE
FOR CONSERVATION

It may be imagined perhaps, that the law has only to declare the right of everyone to what he has himself produced, or acquired by voluntary consent, fairly obtained, of those who produced it. But is there nothing recognized as property except what has been produced? Is there not the earth itself, the forests and waters and all other natural riches above and below the surface? These are the inheritance of the human race, and there must be regulations for the common enjoyment of it. What rights and under what conditions a person shall be allowed to exercise over any portion of this common inheritance cannot be left undecided. No function of government is less optional than the regulation of these things or more completely involved in the idea of civilized Society.

JOHN STUART MILL
Principles of Political Economy

Despite the persistence of certain defects, we have made great social advances in the past several centuries. Even so, such a formidable social achievement as an act of Congress cannot delay the dawn. And no statutory effort, however nobly inspired, can reform man of his love for money. Indeed, so minor a human frailty as the urge to speed is little affected by the law despite the traffic police. There are many forces in this world that cannot be stopped by the law even with hordes of enforcement agents. Of course we must have laws, and we must have police. But it is pointless to squander them on such hopeless tasks as attempting to prevent the private consumption of alcohol, or trying to maintain predetermined prices in the marketplace. The determination of price is *the* function of the commercial market.

How, then, can government tell the market what the price should be?

In theory, the political processes of democracy are independent of, and superior to, the economic processes of the marketplace. So it is clearly the right of government to tell the market what the price *shall* be. At least the government clearly has the right to try. However, there is no substitute for the market in determining what the market price *should* be. So, any price set by law must be either too high or too low—except for occasional accidents like the twice-daily correctness of a stopped clock.

We have had much experience with price-fixing laws in the past, especially during and after World War II. It is well known that these prices by fiat are usually in error. When the price of a particular commodity is too low there is a black market; when the price is too high there is bootlegging. To make matters worse, since bootlegging and the black market are both clearly in violation of the price-fixing laws, an attempt must be made to suppress them. This leads to a never-ending process of investigation, allegation and litigation.

It is indeed unfortunate that the laws of the market are not more amenable to the public will. Were it not for this, one of the most obvious ways of correcting the resource destruction motive might be the easiest. For example, in the case of timber it is undoubtedly in the public interest to restrict cutting to a level slightly below the sustained-yield capacity. If price-fixing were practical, the government could establish, by law, a price so high that consumers would refrain from purchasing more than this sustained-yield amount. Or the government might fix the price so low that the lumber industry would not be stimulated to cut more than the sustained-yield amount. The effects, in either case, should be obvious. With the price too high, the industry would be under great pressure to increase cutting, thereby requiring the presence of enforcement agents everywhere that some trees are still standing. Besides, there would be much incentive to poach and bootleg. If things reached the point where all these possible illegal operations were being carried out in the dark in defiance of a determined enforcement agency, the agents could hardly know at whom they were shooting—producers or consumers. On the other hand, if the price were set low to discourage cutting, a typical black market would spring up in which the black market price would tend to stabilize at, or above, the free market price that would have prevailed for the amount of cutting permitted. So, an elaborate system of priorities, rationing, and allocation would have to be set up in an attempt to control the black market. While this hardly exhausts the unpleasant possibilities it should suffice to show how silly it would be for the government to try to nullify the resource destruction motive by price-fixing.

An attempt to thwart the commercial market by establishing maximum production quotas for natural resource industries would appear to have only slightly more merit than price-fixing. Certainly a considerable amount of enforcement would be required. Also, a great deal of political conniving would emanate from the affected industries. Each corporation that was exploiting some natural resource would seek, through political means, special privileges in the form of larger quotas. And these demands would be supported by the local populace as a way to get more business or more jobs. This pressure would prevent effective production control by state or local governments. So, in the end, it would be necessary that all such controls be centralized in the federal government. That is, the Texas state government could not restrain the private oil producers within its boundaries because of their great political power, and there would be a strong incentive for these private interests to wield their power because of the profits involved. The same conditions would apply, for example, to the lumbering industry in Oregon, the oil interests of Alaska, and the mining industries in many Western states.

It is true that the Texas Railroad Commission regulates oil production in that state. But this commission traditionally regulated production to suit market conditions. Largely through the efforts of one man, the Texas Railroad Commission achieved much in the way of preventing waste; but prevention of waste is only one aspect of long-term conservation. For example, the reader will grant that there is a *fixed* amount of petroleum within the limits of American territory. Now, in 1940, consumption of our petroleum was at an annual rate of 1.35 billion barrels. In 1945, the peak war year, consumption was at the rate of 1.71 billion barrels. In 1965, drain on our *own* oil reserves was at an annual rate of 3.3 billion barrels, while our total demand was 4.2 billion. In 1975, our total consumption was 6 billion barrels. From these data it should be obvious that, even if it were being used efficiently, *petroleum is not being conserved.*

The idea of voluntary conservation, by seeking, through education or persuasion, to limit consumption of scarce natural resources (that is, to convince everybody to voluntarily practice conservation as a moral duty) appears too idealistic for serious consideration. It is doubtful whether history records one instance of a society, or nation, living in complete harmony with nature because of the prudence and sagacity of the individual members of the society. True, the American Indians lived on a self-sustaining basis. Indeed they might have lived that way forever in a permanent American paradise. But there is no reason to suppose that they would have proved wiser and less wasteful than we if it had been they who invented the power saw and the paper dollar. The Indians' use of wampum differed radically from our use of the dollar: they never hoarded teepees full of it; and the possibility of owing forty times as much wampum as there was probably never occurred to them.

Recapitulating, then, any attempt to nullify the resource destruction motive by price control, or by control of private production or consumption obviously would be so difficult, uncertain, and impractical that success by any of these methods would appear extremely doubtful. I conclude, therefore, that this economic enormity we call the resource destruction motive can be cured only by outright public ownership of all natural resources. This is called the "socialization of natural resources." Nationalization is hardly the correct word; for some resources should be owned and managed by state and local governments. The word "socialism" is inappropriate, too, because less than 2% of the total labor force is currently engaged in the process of extracting basic natural resources. The public employment of so small a portion of the labor force wouldn't justify so strong a word as "socialism."

However, the name is not the important thing; it is the result that counts. When, through the efforts of the Audubon Society, migratory waterfowl were taken over by the federal government, the waterfowl were "nationalized" or "socialized." But no matter what it is called, it was the *only way to save these valuable birds from complete annihilation.* No other method would have worked.[1] Whether by accident or not, the only sure cure was the one actually adopted. The results have been most gratifying. So, no matter what it is called, the socialization of natural resources is the only practical way whereby we can save ourselves from the economic bankruptcy and social decline which is the inevitable end point of the resource destruction motive uncontrolled.

There is something that may have escaped your notice in the explanation of the resource destruction motive in Chapters 5 and 6: the same argument that points so clearly and directly toward the public ownership of all those commodities that are uniquely nature's also points toward the *private* ownership of the productive facilities for all those commodities that are *not* uniquely nature's. On the basis of the economics of the resource destruction motive there is no reason for public ownership to encroach any further than the basic natural raw materials. That is, the forests must be publicly owned and managed and the trees must be cut by public enterprise, but the plywood mills and the furniture factories should continue as private enterprise. Likewise, the oil pools of the nation must be publicly owned, but the pipelines and refineries should continue under private ownership.

Moreover, some compromise may be permitted for those basic natural materials that are so abundant that the operation of the

---

[1] Please note that it was not necessary to remove waterfowl entirely from the market, so long as they are publicly owned and harvested on a sustained-yield basis. That is, the number now shot by sportsmen could be harvested by government hunters and sold for food in the market without bringing about annihilation.

resource destruction motive is only a remote possibility. For example, limestone, sandstone and cement rock quarries, oil shale deposits, pottery clay, glass sands, abundant low-grade ores, etc., might remain in private hands. In these cases, however, it must be made clear, by law, that the private operators are merely holding these resources in trust for the people, and that full responsibility is associated with this trusteeship. There must be no "creaming" of mines, no destruction of arable land or of scenic beauty, no fouling of the air or water. In short, the private exploitation of any abundant resource must be carried out in complete harmony with the interests of the public at large.

Now, as to the sale of publicly owned materials to private industry, it should be recognized that the public must sell those natural commodities that it wishes to send to market *at the market price:* to the highest bidder, that is. Remember, the commercial market sets the price. If the public offered a resource commodity at some lower price, the original purchasers merely would resell at the free market price and pocket an unearned profit (a black market). This profit would be of much more value to the community at large if it were collected by the government and spent on conservation measures.

It should be obvious that the public will send to market slightly less than the sustained-yield amount of those resources that are renewable—timber, fur bearers, fish, etc. Such a practice would permit a gradual increase in these commodities by natural growth and, consequently, a steady expansion of the potential rate of consumption. For non-renewable resources, such as petroleum and ores, perpetually available supplies are not possible if there is a constant or increasing rate of consumption. But suppose that the public permitted not more than one percent (for example) of the remaining reserves of any non-replaceable resource to go to market. When, then, would the supply become exhausted? The answer is "never." You see, we would then *always* have reserves enough for 100 years at the current year's rate of consumption. Look at it this way: if you had 1,000 pounds of coal and each year you burned no more than 10% of your remaining reserve—100 pounds the first year, 90 pounds the second,

81 pounds the third, etc., you would never exhaust your supply of coal. In fact you would always have a reserve equal to a 10-year supply at the rate of use during the most recent year.

The practice of making gradually decreasing supplies of non-renewable natural resources available to the economy would strongly stimulate the orderly development of substitutes, more efficient usage, and salvage and re-use methods. These latter important aspects of conservation should develop quite satisfactorily under private enterprise. So it is quite possible that, with the public acquisition of our natural resources, and the subsequent consumption of them on a sustained-yield basis for those that are renewable and on a percentage-of-the-remaining-reserve basis for those that are non-renewable, we would have within our grasp a practicable perpetual economy.

Now, there are no really serious obstacles in the way of socializing our natural resources. England, France, the Scandinavian countries, even India, found it fairly easy to nationalize large important segments of their economies. Mexico nationalized its petroleum resources many years ago. In the light of such actual occurrences elsewhere, it would be silly to think that we would find the socialization of natural resources to be impossibly difficult.

The public acquisition of natural resources can, and should, be an orderly affair. Forests, petroleum, and natural gas first, because of the urgency. Then the scarcer ores, marine resources and coal. The wildlife, fur-bearers and freshwater fish, already are in the public domain. In fact, about one-fourth of the land area of the country is still under public ownership. This gives us a good start. For example, some timber, oil and ore resources currently being exploited for profit can be recaptured simply by terminating leases.

Let us consider the acquisition of timberland as a specific example. About 50% of America's sawtimber (on a board-foot basis) is still publicly owned. Actually only about 30% of the timberland is publicly owned. But the private timberland has been cut-over so heavily under the resource destruction motive that the volume of public sawtimber looms larger percentagewise. However, we can say—and it's nice to be able to say it—that about one-third of the forest land (in terms of value) already is publicly owned.

Another 30% of the timberland (by value) is on farms. The smaller farm timber plots should remain under the farmer's ownership and management to supply his own and some local needs. But where the farm timberlands are of substantial acreage they should become part of the public's resources. These could be acquired under long-term lease. So, we could do both the farmer and the public at large a good turn at a cost probably no greater than the present rate of public expenditure for farm subsidies.

This leaves us less than half of the nation's timber resources (about 40% of the timberland and 30% of the actual sawtimber volume) that must be purchased outright. The purchase of this land at a price based on fair value could be accomplished through the insurance technique. The insurance companies would buy the land with insurance policies and certificates, then sell to the government (state or federal) on a rental-applied-to-purchase-price basis. The government would pay the rental-purchase payments out of operating surplus. You see, the public will cut on a sustained-yield basis, and sell to the highest private bidder. The surplus of receipts over costs under these managed conditions should be quite adequate.

Of course, it would be possible to socialize natural resources even without the insurance technique. As has been mentioned above, many other countries have nationalized all sorts of private industries and properties. The point is that nationalization is not unusual under any given conditions. Under the insurance technique it could be both orderly and practicable.

The problems of acquiring the other natural resources—petroleum, coal, ore bodies, etc.—will not differ greatly from the problem of recapturing our forests. Mineral rights under the farmers' lands, for example, could be acquired by lease and royalty payments, thus giving the farmer another boost toward "parity" status in the economy.

Strange as it may seem, then, this worst-of-all defect in the present economy is fairly easily cured. Once the majority of Americans decide that these natural resources so essential to our future must be taken under public ownership in order to nullify the resource destruction motive, no serious obstacles stand in the way of buying and paying for them. There are many dangers we face that cannot be banished by the simple process of buying our way out. The resource destruction motive, fortunately, is of a different nature. Release from this greatest economic danger—the rapid impoverishment of an entire nation by a merciless economic force—is for sale, and at a bargain price.

9

A MEMORANDUM ON A PRACTICABLE COMPOSITE ECONOMY

> The social problem of the future we considered to be, how to unite the greatest individual liberty of action with the common ownership of the raw material of the globe, and an equal participation of all in the benefits of combined labor.
>
> JOHN STUART MILL
> *Autobiography*

It is the purpose of this memorandum to show: (1) that the existing categories of business enterprise can be reformed and composed into a new economy; and (2) that this new economy will be lacking in those great faults of the present economy which, as we have seen, can lead only to economic chaos and social decline.

That such reform is needed has been argued at length in the preceding text. In the end, however, the need for reform will be proved not by argument but by the real world. Eventually, an actual emergency will prove it beyond all doubt. When that time comes, a plan for a new economy that is composed of reformed *existing* economic institutions should be more practicable than some other idea. Outlined below is a plan for such a Composite Economy and its categories of enterprise.

CATEGORY I: COMPETITIVE ENTERPRISE

Perhaps no type of business organization is nearer the ideals of American democracy than private competitive enterprise. For-

156 A New Economy

tunately this type of enterprise will be larger and more important in the Composite Economy than in the existing economy. Indeed, the more competitive enterprise there is (excepting the harvest of natural resources), the better the Composite Economy will be.

In this memorandum, private competitive enterprise is defined as all enterprises that will tend to operate at or near capacity whether the owners are getting richer in the process or not. This definition is more inclusive than it first appears. It will embrace all the smaller farms, shops, mills, bakeries, garages, etc.; all the individual "independent contractors" (doctors, dentists, lawyers, barbers, architects, etc.); all non-profit enterprises such as colleges, hospitals and church organizations; and most cooperatives and mutual-ownership activities. In general, if an enterprise is non-corporate, mutual, cooperative or non-profit, it will meet this definition.

In the study of the farm problem, we saw that the case for owner-operated family-size farms is impressive. We saw, too, that the case *against* absentee-owned and factory-size farms is even more impressive. It is important, then, that agriculture in the composite economy is owner-operated in fairly small units. And it will be necessary to accomplish this by democratic action. It may surprise you that in our capitalistic economy it is necessary to *restore* private competitive enterprise by deliberate public action. But economic history clearly shows that *laissez-faire*—letting things drift—is not favorable to truly competitive enterprise. This is especially glaring as it applies to land ownership. In country after country—Italy, Iran, Egypt, China, India, and many in Latin America—we have seen land reform carried out only after long periods of injustice or social decline. Actually our country already has passed through two periods when some land reform was carried out. First, after the Revolution, the baronial estates (Royal grants) were seized and subdivided. In those days, 50 or 100 acres was judged the right size for a family farm. Later, the Homestead Act of 1862 set a size of 160 acres for a family farm, and 250 million acres of public domain were so distributed. *In the long run, in every country it is necessary to carry out land reform either by revolution or governmental action.* We have already used each method in carrying out some land reform.

The guiding principle for land reform under the Composite Economy will be Taussig's dictum: "The most wholesome conditions for agriculture are a wide diffusion of ownership of arable land and a predominance of cultivation by the owners." This will assure full, steady production, both short-run and long-run, and provide favorable conditions for soil conservation. In the Composite Economy then, all arable land will be in family-size farms. The size should not exceed, say, 300 to 600 acres. Units larger than the limits finally decided upon will be subdivided. Then, together with all absentee and corporate holdings, these family-size units will be placed in the hands of genuine farmers for operation under their ownership.

Now, an old argument can be used against land reform: "Big business is big because it is efficient." Usually, this is a hollow argument since the proponent means: efficient in making money. This is not the same as the efficiency arising from maximum output at minimum cost. Nor does it imply the social optimum. In farming, however, efficiency in making money (except for the government subsidy) does come mainly from efficient operation. The big farm must sell at the same market price as does the small farm. So, if big farms make a profit when small farms don't, then the big farms are more efficient in the common meaning of the word. At present, this is actually often the case.

Would we, then, gain wholesome conditions through land reform but lose efficiency? Would we gain steady production at the cost of reduced production? Would we gain long-range productivity at the cost of higher prices? To each question the answer is: not necessarily. In principle, the small enterpriser strives to maximize output at the point of least average cost, and to sell at a price equal to marginal cost. Land reform, by increasing the extent of competitive enterprise, would make this principle more widely applicable rather than less. So, overall long-term efficiency should actually increase. And there is an actual historical example of this effect in the rigorous Japanese land reform of the 1870s. There, the peasants who became farmers soon more than doubled farm output and thereby helped greatly the subsequent industrial growth of Japan.

If factory-size farms now are making profits when family-size farms aren't, it is often because the big farms have made some monopolistic gain.[1] Many of them use wetbacks or other exploited labor. Also they are better set up to take advantage of government subsidy money. Some of them reduce output (and lay off their workers) when prices are unfavorable. The larger ones can get financing at lower interest rates—or, by paying cash for farm machinery, escape interest charges entirely. Determining the full extent of these monopolistic gains would require much research. But, really, this matter is largely irrelevant. You see, for years we have been deliberately trying to *reduce* farm production. In the new economy, this policy of "payment not to produce" will be abolished. So, farm output would be higher, not lower. Then, too, farm costs will be reduced by the elimination of interest payments. So, food prices (since they will tend toward marginal cost) might well decline rather than rise.

Further, two very important aspects of modern agriculture—mechanization and research—both favor return to family-size farms. Modern farm machinery permits a larger, more productive *and* more remunerative, family-size farm. Under the insurance technique this machinery would be easier to acquire (by rental-purchase without interest) both by small farmers, and by farm co-ops, than at present.

In industry, research is carried out by the big corporations. This tends to give them an aura of indispensability. Such is not the case in agriculture. Most agricultural research is carried out at public expense by government agencies and in universities. The results are passed on to all farmers—and everyone benefits. This arrangement would not be harmed by the abolishment of factory-size farms.

---

[1]One actual example: During the California tax scandals of 1965 it was disclosed that one corporate farm was evading $4 million per year in property taxes. Only a big business can engage in fraud on this scale. Small farmers simply can't afford to bribe tax assessors.

Nor do the financial arrangements for carrying out land reform present any insurmountable problems. Oversize and absentee or corporate-owned holdings would be purchased by the insurance companies in the manner described in Chapter 8. Then, after subdivision, the family-size parcels would be sold to bonafide farmers on a rental-purchase basis. Further, if existing debt is transferred to non-debt form rather than cancelled outright, unpaid farm mortgages could be taken over by the insurance companies. The mortgage holders would exchange them for insurance policies or certificates. The present tenants would then acquire ownership by completing the payments on a rental-purchase basis.

Thus, the competitive-enterprise category is prepared for its role in the Composite Economy. It is simply *land reform:* a relatively few too-large holdings will be broken up into a larger number of moderate-size farms, all to be owned and occupied by the operators.

Of course, some people will call this revolutionary; others will consider it quite unorthodox. The former mistake cause for effect: land reform is often associated with revolution because if the need for land reform is let go too long it can bring on revolution. Admittedly the proposal to do it now *is* unorthodox: the usual way is to let matters grow worse until social repercussions occur.

Actually, the earlier it is done the easier it will be. If such reform were carried out in the 1970s, for example, it would not be far from nipping matters in the bud. About 200,000 outsize farms would have to be acquired. These would be subdivided into about 700,000 family farms. Thus the number of farms in the country would be increased by 500,000: an increase of only about 15%. So, it would be reform, not revolution.

After restoring farming to a competitive status, however, it will be necessary to support it against monopolistic pressure. In the Composite Economy there will be no subsidy payments simply for not producing. But the farmers would own valuable assets needed by the country at large, such as timber plots, mineral rights and hunting and fishing rights. These could be leased from the farmers on long-term basis. Thus the public would acquire assets necessary for a perpetual economy, while the farmer would receive a steady income over and above his under-par income from competitive enterprise farming.

It will not be necessary to break up the big-business food manufacturers into smaller competitive units in order to solve the food problem. The danger of reduction of food production by these big-business processors can be prevented by establishing minimum production quotas. Since the food problem is ripe to break upon us early in a depression and without much warning, the simplest and quickest solution must be chosen. Eventually, under the Composite Economy the food problem should pass away along with depressions.

CATEGORY II:
PRIVATE ENTERPRISE UNDER PUBLIC CONTROL

Let us begin this by recognizing that a large part of our economy already operates under some public control. Consider the federal crop controls which are imposed on competitive enterprises (i.e., small farmers). Beyond this, there are the publicly regulated big-business enterprises: railroads, telephone, power and gas corporations; the banks and insurance companies, security exchanges, airlines, telegraph, radio, television, etc.

It is safe to assume that most of the controls now in effect have some economic justification. That is, practically every control is a democratic response to some problem arising in the existing economy. The myriads of laws and regulations that we have found necessary to impose on the business community stand as a frightful indictment of American capitalism and its deep-seated defects. You see, in addition to the monetary shortfall and the resource destruction motive, there is in American capitalism a pronounced tendency toward monopoly. In the past, few of our legislators understood the cause of "boom and bust"; fewer still were familiar with the devastating effects of the resource destruction motive. So, it is not surprising that the economic controls now in force do little in the way of correcting these two worst faults in the present system. Nor has the growth of monopolistic enterprise been arrested. But we all recognize outright monopoly. Despite our aversion for government controls over business, our record in regulation of obvious forms of monopoly (e.g., public utilities) is not bad at all.

The crux of the present public control over these utilities is this: their annual profit is limited, by law, to a fixed percentage of the value of their investment. Though subject to some abuse it does prevent them from grossly overcharging. On the other hand it encourages them to invest heavily in plant and equipment. But expensive plant and equipment is a good place for private investment! According to Keynes, the more the private owners of capital *invest* their money the better it is for the country as a whole. So, expensive power plants, telephone exchanges, etc., are really better for the community than cheaply constructed ones. Besides, these high-cost investments tend to be quite efficient in operation.

In the Composite Economy, then, these utilities will remain as they are: privately owned but under public control. Indeed, according to the economic reasoning on which the Composite Economy is based, these utilities *should* be privately owned as should some that are now publicly owned, like the postal service and the TVA. Of course, since the Composite Economy is to be relatively debt-free, the bonded debt of all public utilities is to be redeemed by preferred stock: a reform that will also greatly reduce their risk of bankruptcy.

The central nervous system of the Composite Economy will be the insurance technique, which will operate through private insurance companies under public control, plus a central monetary authority. Since insurance companies already are under public control, the insurance technique will not require a net addition to the public-control category. Rather, there will be a novel change in operation. In addition, since the insurance technique will provide for investment and saving *without* debt, about three trillion dollars of burdensome existing debt will be changed into non-debt form. All this, of course, is stronger stuff than the generally ineffectual economic reforms of the past.

These substantial reforms are necessary because of a terrible defect in the existing economy: the monetary shortfall. This defect exists because the owners of large blocks of capital refrain from spending and investing all their income. As money circulates, each time a dollar gets in the hands of one of these fellows he keeps part of it (about 10%). And the next time it comes around to him he keeps another 10%. If these fellows hoarded all their accumulated profits, the total currency supply would disappear in less than a year—and the whole economy could be stopped dead. However, the accumulators generally lend their captured money: provided, of course, that the borrowers promise to pay the money back and, in addition, pay interest.

We might add that the accumulators generally lend out their captured money, provided someone *agrees to borrow it*. You see, the rich owners of capital have incomes in excess of all they wish to spend for consumption and investment. The remainder is available for lending. But, if no one borrowed it, it would automatically become a hoard. Usually, however, the money does get borrowed.

The borrower normally borrows money only to spend or invest it. When the money is spent or invested it goes to buy the products of existing capital. So, the borrowed money gets back to the original lenders as the yield on the capital they own. In practice this process is repeated again and again as the money supply turns over. And the loans and debts grow higher and higher. But note: even after the very first turnover the lenders *have* the money that the borrowers owe them. If at this point the lender demanded payment of the loan he might perceive a little-known fact about debt: in the aggregate it cannot be repaid. Even so, the process continues until the borrowers refuse to borrow more; or the lenders refuse to lend; or, as a mathematical finality, the interest charges equal the borrowers' income. So, the lending of money merely delays the day when the rich finally must hoard their excess income for want of anything else to do with it. At that point, the economic life of the nation would come to a halt.

Of course, American capitalism has grown to its present size under these conditions. In its early stages the parcels of capital were so small that the profits did not produce greatly excessive incomes. This was the private competitive enterprise stage. But after a while the reinvestment of profits increased the power of the owners and brought them incomes larger than they wished to use for spending and investment. And so began a series of panics and depressions that culminated in the great depression of 1929-40. The earlier panics and depressions may actually have helped the growth of the country: when people were disemployed by the owners of capital in the industrial East they simply moved west. But, as the country and the economy matured, the restrictive bands of bad monetary habits pressed tighter and tighter, threatening to strangle the whole system.

In recent times (1941-75) the economy has been artificially maintained by public and private debt expanding so fast that existing capital is bringing in so much profit for accumulation that investment in more capital is encouraged. In addition, repeated waves of inflation, sponsored by the government through the banking and monetary system, tend to reduce the weight of older debts. But these are only temporary expedients. They only postpone the inevitable: the expansion of debt must one day come to an end, and with it the end of prosperity.

The Composite Economy proposes to escape this monetary death trap by a novel financial technique that will practically insure that *all* incomes are actually paid out either for consumption or investment (for future consumption). This new mode of financial conduct will recognize and fulfill the desire of individuals to save. It will eliminate lending by making borrowing unnecessary. It will discourage hoarding by removing most reasons for hoarding. Of course, this new technique will not be perfect. But, as we shall see, it has many practical aspects in its favor. First, however, we will run through an example of the technique, following one particular income along its course. Later we will examine the reasons for, and the advantages of, each particular phase.

For the example, we will use an individual income of $100,-000. In the existing economy, anyone who admits $100,000 income pays about $50,000 to the government, while $50,000 is take-home pay. Since the government always spends or invests all *its* income, it is the take-home income that gives rise to the monetary shortfall. A part of this income will be spent for consumption. Another part—the size of which varies with the changes in business confidence and credit conditions—will be invested. A third portion will be lent (including depositing in banks or "buying" insurance). A fourth portion might be hoarded. It is the latter two portions that cause the monetary shortfall and, eventually, financial collapse.

Under the new technique an income of $100,000 will be taxed only about 25% (based on the needs of the government, not on the need to correct the maldistribution of income). About $25,000 will be allowed for take-home pay (spending)—based on the assumption that most $100,000 income families could spend $25,000 without resorting to antisocial or uneconomic outlets. The remaining $50,000, although collected by the government along with the income tax, will be turned over as premium payments in the name of the individual, to an insurance company of his choice. The insurance company will issue to the individual $50,000 worth of insurance policies and certificates. These policies and certificates will be the individual's savings.

The insurance company will now pay out the $50,000 to build, for example, a new house, a new school bus and a new drilling machine. The house will be rented (sold) to a family who will make payments (that exclude interest) until the price of the house (including all expenses except interest) is paid. The school bus will be rented (sold) to a public school district which will pay, out of its tax receipts, by the month or year until the bus is paid for. The drilling machine will be purchased by a manufacturer, paying by the month until he owns it outright.

As these rental payments flow back to the insurance company they will be used to pay any claims the insurance holder (saver) may have for fire, theft, sickness, hospital, accident, business failure or other financial loss, retirement, etc., etc. If no misfortunes have befallen the saver, the rental receipts will be reinvested in other durable assets to be sold by rental-applied-to-purchases-price. No one needs sign a mortgage to own a house, issue bonds to buy school buses, or borrow at the bank to buy new capital goods.

That's all there is to the basic mechanism of the insurance technique. It is easy to see just from this example how savings are turned into investments, but the reverse process deserves a brief review. First, note that each dollar of the original premium payments keeps returning to the insurance company until it is needed to pay a claim. Thus it is truly "saved," for it is available when it is really needed by the saver. Indeed, any time a person who has saved money for a possible future need, or feared misfortune, finds that the time has come, he will discover that it is not really money that is needed but, rather, something that money will buy. For example, if a person is suddenly stricken ill, currency can do him no good; but the services of an *existing* hospital could. And a hospital is an investment. So you see we can provide for future needs only by investing now. This is precisely what the insurance technique does. In the present economy individual "saving" finds its way into investment only imperfectly and by accident when it is lent, and not at all when it is hoarded. Besides, if it is lent there is serious doubt whether it can be paid back when the saver needs it most.

Now, the control that will be exercised over the insurance companies will include the requirement that their investments be made in an amount equal to the funds not needed for current claims, and that these investments be sold on a rental-applied-to-purchase-price basis *without interest*. The type of actual investments, whether buildings, factories, schools, etc., will be decided by the insurance companies. Therefore, the investments will be made in those capital or durable assets most likely to return their full cost. In addition, savers of insurance certificates will be entitled to redeem them for any capital assets they wish. For example, an enterpriser may interest certain well-to-do men in a new industry. Upon forming a corporation the investors will turn in their insurance certificates (i.e., savings) for stock. The new corporation will buy its new plant and equipment by turning in the certificates to the insurance company. In this case no rental-purchase payments will be involved. The corporation will own the capital outright (i.e., a direct exchange of insurance certificates for capital). So, the actual choice of just what capital or durable assets are to be created will be decided by the insurance companies or private individuals. It is not quite accurate, therefore, to call the insurance technique the "socialization of investment" as Keynes used the term. True, society makes the rules—that is, it will insist that the savings of the nation are turned into investment. But private business will play the game—that is, decide what investments are to be made.

In a strict economic sense, investment is not only a true form of saving; it is the *only* true form of saving. So, it is quite sound for the community at large to require that the savings of the nation are invested. The next step is to make the total of excess incomes of the nation actually flow into the insurance companies. It is intended to achieve this phase of the technique through the federal income tax collection system: by collecting the insurance assessment right along with the tax. This will be done in such a way that there will be incentive for the payment of both tax and assessment.

With its present rate structure the income tax system, though it has some basis in economic theory, is socially obnoxious and seems always at the point of incipient breakdown. Small wonder: a man with an income of $500,000 a year is supposed to pay a tax of about $320,000 and keep about $180,000. This is all wrong. In the first place, 65% of a man's income is too much to confiscate. In the second place, $180,000 is too much cash to leave in the hands of one individual, for it most certainly won't all be spent or invested. In the third place, the taxpayer would probably find a way to evade the $320,000 tax in the first place.

Tax rates under the insurance technique will be progressive too, but will reach a maximum at about 30% on million-dollar incomes. So they will be much less steeply progressive than at present. "Take-home" income left to an individual with an income of $1,000,000 will amount to about $80,000. The remainder will be the insurance assessment (savings). Under these rates an individual income of $1,000,000 will be allocated as tabulated below:

		Under the Insurance Technique
Under the Present System		
$685,000	Income tax	$300,000
$315,000	Take-home income	$ 80,000
—0—	Insurance assessment	$620,000 (savings)

A comparison of the rates under the insurance technique with the nearly intolerable tax rates under the present system should clearly disclose the fundamental difference—especially to the taxpayer: the government *saving* a large part of a man's income for him is obviously preferable to the government *spending* it for him. This collection system of the insurance technique may be called "socialization of savings." A taxpayer saves by declaring his full income and paying his full savings assessment. True, as his income increases his taxes increase. But his savings increase at a faster rate. This latter feature adds some incentive to declare, and pay, the full assessment.

Once free of existing debt (see Chapter 7) we can except the Composite Economy to remain relatively free of debt without a lot of laws or regulations. You see, the insurance companies will be investing the nation's savings in capital and durable assets such as industrial facilities, schools, turnpikes, houses, etc. These are the types of assets which, in the present economy, require corporate bonds, business loans, public bond issues and mortgage debt. It is unlikely that anyone would wish to go into debt and pay interest when it is not necessary to do so.

*   *   *

The Composite Economy will not be completely debt-free; only relatively so when compared with the existing order. By 1976, net public and private debt exceeded $3,000 billion. If the insurance technique were in effect at that time, total debt would have been no greater than $200 billion and perhaps as little as $75 billion. You see, the Composite Economy will eliminate most of the debt along with its heavy burden of interest. It will not eliminate the interest rate or the need to pay interest on some monetary savings.

Primarily, money is a medium of exchange. But money can also be stored for possible future purposes. This quality gives rise to hoarding by people who, by nature, are concerned about their possible future need for things that money can buy. The more concerned they are, the more solace is derived from having the money at hand. Interest is the reward that these people require for giving up their comforting liquidity. The real rate of interest (after deducting the rate of inflation) measures their reluctance to give it up.

Money and people, then, being what they are, there will always be a positive real rate of interest—something above 0%—required to prevent hoarding. We have seen that neither hoarding nor lending provide satisfactory forms of saving. But how can we convince a person who has money that he does not wish to spend or invest that he should neither hoard nor lend? In the absence of some clever device that would render money unfit for purposes other than conducting current business, there will always be some urge to hoard; and the need for a positive rate of interest to counter it. Of course, hoarding does one economic service in providing solace. In any event, this urge to hoard remains a stubborn barrier standing in the way of economic perfection.

The Composite Economy is not designed to meet this problem head-on. The savings and tax assessments levied on individual incomes as part of the insurance technique are intended to prevent excessive take-home incomes. So, it won't be easy for large amounts to be hoarded or lent. The insurance policies and certificates issued in exchange for the savings assessments are intended to allay disquietude about the future. So, restrictive forces, hitherto non-existent, will be acting on the *ability* to hoard and the *urge* to hoard. To learn the effectiveness of these new things we must await actual experience.

In addition, it seems practical to require the insurance companies to carry out their investments in a manner that will tend to stabilize prices. Large volumes of investment will be underway at all times. By increasing the tempo of work when prices are tending too low and decreasing the tempo when prices are tending too high, some stability of prices could be achieved. This price stability would eliminate one more of the common reasons for hoarding—the speculative motive.

But, so long as there is money, there will exist a desire to hoard and, as a result, a rate of interest. The going rate will be determined largely by psychological forces when the economic forces affecting the desire to hoard are relatively stable. But if interest is the reward for not hoarding, then, in logic, total debt should not exceed an amount equal to the supply of currency. That is, lenders should not be getting a reward for *not* hoarding *more* than the total supply of legal money. It so happens that, under the Composite Economy, the banking system could be regulated by the reserve requirements so that this maximum amount of debt is provided for. You see, if the legal reserve requirement on deposits was set at 50%, the banking system could make, at the most, loans equal in amount to the supply of currency; and it could accept, at the most, deposits in the amount of two times the supply of currency.

Of course, this is something of a compromise. But a banking system exists and provides important services. That the system currently owes its depositors ten times the total supply of legal money is the result of an average reserve requirement of only about 10%. For perfect solvency, cash reserves would have to be 100%. This would prevent the making of loans, the payment of interest, and the expansion of the currency into a larger amount of checkbook money. For the Composite Economy, however, the only basic change in the banking system is to be the raising of the cash reserve requirement to about 50%.

Actually, this increase in reserves will have the effect of reducing the relative financial importance of the banking system. That is, within the Composite Economy, insurance companies will be much more important and banks much less. The banking system will, in fact, be reduced to about a third of its present importance. And yet many banking functions will remain just as essential as they are under the old economy: checking account services, letters of credit and acceptances, savings and safe deposit services, etc. Of course banks will also make loans and receive interest. Mainly these will be short-term business and consumer loans which the larger insurance companies would find inconvenient as an outlet for their investment funds.

CATEGORY III: PUBLIC ENTERPRISE

The smallest of the four main categories in the Composite Economy, comprising less than 10% of the total productive economic effort of the nation, is to be public enterprise. This is defined as any enterprise producing goods or services *for sale* which is owned and operated by the federal government or any political subdivision—i.e., state, municipal, public authority, etc. The most obvious example in the existing economy is the postal service; other examples are the TVA, toll roads, city-owned water systems, etc. But it is not these things with which the Composite Economy is concerned. Public enterprise under the new economy will involve the very foundation of the nation's economic life: natural resources.

"The requisites of production," wrote John Stuart Mill, "are two: labour, and suitable natural objects." For production to continue indefinitely, there must be a perpetual supply of suitable natural objects. If the supply of a particular natural resource is depleted, so, eventually, must be the supply of those commodities produced from it. This is not to suggest that the entire earth can be consumed. But the economic well-being of any society in any age depends upon certain natural resources that are absolutely essential. And nature does not guarantee to supply precisely those resources that are needed for as long as they are needed.

Obviously it is the responsibility of society, not of nature, to see that the supply of essential natural objects does not become deficient.

This brings up the question of just how these natural resources can be harvested without, as a consequence, bringing about their exhaustion. Luckily this is not a difficult question, in theory at least. For those natural resources that are renewable—forests, fish, etc.—we shall harvest them at a rate not exceeding the rate at which nature is replenishing the supply: the sustained-yield capacity. If thus harvested, the basic supply could remain undiminished. For those resources that are non-renewable, such as ores, coal and petroleum, we will not extract them at a rate higher than a small fixed percentage of the remaining reserves. For example, suppose the total recoverable deposits of an important ore amount to 10,000,000 tons, and it is desired always to have a hundred years' supply. If, then, not more than 1% of the amount of the ore *remaining* is marketed each year (i.e., 100,000 tons the first year, 99,000 tons the second year, 98,010 tons the third year and so on), there *always* will be an ore reserve one hundred times as much as the current year's use. This plan of consumption on a percentage-of-the-remaining-reserve basis will provide for a slowly decreasing supply reaching the market. So, it will encourage the orderly development of recycling, more efficient use, development of substitutes, finding new reserves or arranging for imports.

In principle, then, it is quite simple to devise maximum annual rates of consumption for our natural resources which would make possible the perpetual availability of those essential things on which our economic life depends. In our present economy however, there are powerful forces acting not only to prevent the proper use of our resources but to produce just the opposite effect. If a natural resource is being depleted its price will rise as it becomes scarcer. As the price rises, more industrial effort is exerted to market the resource faster. Thus it is made scarcer still. So, its price will rise once more. This is the resource destruction motive.

The main drive of privately owned industry is toward maximum profit. In the extraction or harvesting of natural resources the maximum profits accrue from sending them to market when the price is high or rising. Not only does the drive for profits override any concern about the exhaustion of the resource but as the resource gets scarcer the price goes higher. Obviously, then, our society's need for perpetual supplies of natural re-

sources and the drive of private industry to exhaust the supplies
are in conflict. So, either the economic life of our society must
decline for lack of essential natural objects—or the ownership
of natural resources must be removed from private hands. In
the Composite Economy all natural resources, except those
copiously abundant, will be publicly owned. And the harvesting
of these resources will be on a sustained-yield or percentage-of-
remaining-reserve basis.

However, in the Composite Economy public enterprise will be
limited to the natural resource industries—lumbering, mining,
fishing, etc. You see, the same economic forces which, under
private industry, motivate the exhaustion of natural resources
also motivate the *production* of commercial commodities. Consider, for example, two such practically identical items as wild-
mink coats and ranch-mink coats and assume a rise in price takes
place for both. Greater effort will be directed to trapping wild
mink which, though it may provide for a few additional coats in
the short run, will reduce the natural stock of breeding mink so
that, in the end, the number of coats reaching market will be
decreased. The price rise for ranch-mink coats, on the other hand,
will stimulate production all along the line: the profits accruing
from the higher price will motivate the expansion of mink
ranches or the establishment of new ones so that, in the end, the
number of ranch-mink coats will be increased. So, the same economic forces have produced opposite effects: desirable ones in
the case of the commercial item; appalling ones in the case of
the natural one because, upon further thought, it can be seen
that the first reduction in supply brought about by the first price
rise will induce another rise in price and another reduction in
supply.

Public acquisition of the nation's natural resources (some, of
course, already are publicly owned—notably wildlife, fish, much
forest land and some ores and petroleum) is to be accomplished
by purchase by the insurance companies and resale to the government on a rental-applied-to-purchase-price basis. The particular government (state, federal or local) in which ownership is
vested and the particular public agency that operates them is

largely a political question and is of no singular importance in
the Composite Economy so long as some central agency—perhaps
a Federal Department of Conservation—is charged with regulating the aggregate harvest in the interest of the public welfare.
While the emphasis will be on the public good rather than
profits, the supply of resources available for marketing will be
sold in the commercial market at the price determined by supply
and demand. Profits arising from the operations will be used for
payments of the rental-applied-to-purchase-price, conservation
operations and general public funds.

❖   ❖   ❖

The extent, and the role, of public enterprise in the Composite
Economy is quite clearly defined by the economic consequences
of the resource destruction motive. That is, public ownership
and operation of the basic natural resource industries constitute a specific solution of a specific problem: the inevitable
depletion of natural resources under private business ownership.
At present, under the existing order, there is no such guiding
economic principle upon which the scope of public enterprise
is based.

It is truly amazing how many schools of thought there are on
government ownership. The communists would have practically
everything owned by the state, and believe the collapse of capitalism both inevitable and desirable. Socialists are more prag-
matic, and much more diverse. At the mildest level they would
have the state provide schools, roads, communications and
power, arguing that industry could not be productive without
these basic services. This is reasonable enough, but *we* have
excellent communications and power supply: both provided by
private industry.

Most socialists would insist that the "war" industry, at least,
should be government-owned. That owners of capital get rich
while the people suffer the rigors of war seems reason enough
for this. Many socialists would go further, socializing most all
heavy industry, hoping to end the imperialist struggle to gain a

favorable foreign trade income. But the Composite Economy wouldn't need war or war debt or favorable trade income to maintain prosperity; there could be no war millionaires if there were no war debt, and there would be no economic necessity for imperialistic trade.

Some economists argue that publicly owned heavy industry could be a useful tool in fighting depressions since investment could be *increased* when the economy is declining. This idea was expressed by Slichter, a Harvard economist, in his book *The American Economy*. Unfortunately, as shown in Chapter 2, our present economy needs expanding debt in *addition* to high rates of investment in order to maintain prosperity. So, if we embarked on socializing industry to prevent depressions by increasing investment we would end up socializing *all* industry before a stable economy could be achieved. It would be better to socialize only the investment aspect as suggested by Keynes. But it would be equally effective to socialize only savings: the other side of the investment coin.

Economists who study the pros and cons of different economic systems are generally critical of wasteful practices in the extractive industries in capitalist economies. In mining, the most profitable seams of ore or coal are removed, leaving behind the less profitable, perhaps never to be recovered. Forests are "clear-cut", or timbered by the "cut and run" method. Wastes, pollutants and poisons are disposed of the cheapest way, not the safest. And on and on. These economists, though not themselves socialists, point out that these predatory practices would be abated by social ownership. Of course, these problems would be solved by the Composite Economy since natural resources *will* be publicly owned, albeit for a different reason.

It would be unseemly to claim that the resource destruction motive is the only compelling reason for socializing natural resources. Nor will the Composite Economy prevent the people from socializing other segments of the American economy. But the economic reasoning on which the Composite Economy is based clearly proves the necessity for public ownership of natural resources. It also clearly indicates the exclusion of public ownership from other fields of production.

CATEGORY IV: MONOPOLISTIC ENTERPRISE

The largest of the four categories of business enterprise in the Composite Economy (it is also the largest segment of the existing economy) will be monopolistic enterprise. It is defined as all those private enterprises (except those under public control) that will not operate at or near full capacity unless the private owners are getting richer in the process. In short—big business.

This is the type of business enterprise mainly responsible for the monetary shortfall. But the term "monopolistic" is used for economic accuracy, not opprobrium. Of course, there are those who claim that big business *is* competitive. But in economics "competition" requires that there be many buyers and many sellers. Of potatoes, for example, both buyers and sellers are numbered in the millions. Of automobiles the buyers outnumber the sellers by a million to one. Obviously, the one adjective "competitive" does not apply in a scientifically useful sense to both. In economic literature the terms "monopolistic competition," "oligopoly" and "imperfect competition" are applied to big business. But in this memorandum, "monopolistic" is used and means, roughly, big business.

There are really three aspects of American big business that disqualify it from being classified as competitive enterprise. First, of course, is the fact that there are few sellers for many buyers. For example, the heads of those corporations that produce over half of the total national product could be seated in your local theater. This is a situation vastly different from that upon which Adam Smith based his plea for *laissez-faire*. Really, this is a matter of much more import than mere definition of terms. Without many sellers for the many buyers the theoretical basis for private enterprise is largely swept away: the economic forces that promote efficiency, establish just prices and prevent misuse of economic power *do not exist*. Unfortunately, these tendencies toward industrial inefficiency, unjust prices and misuse of power also will be present, though somewhat mitigated, in the Composite Economy. So, if they are not intolerable now, certainly they will not be in the Composite Economy.

Another monopolistic aspect of big business derives from its ability to obtain the desired profit. Of course, even a potato farmer tries for the maximum net return. But he must achieve this by producing at the lowest average unit cost (i.e., maximum efficiency). You see, his contribution to the market, whether 50 bushels or 5,000 bushels, has little effect on supply or, therefore, price. An individual competitive enterpriser, since he can't affect the *total* supply, never can achieve monopolistic price. But a big corporation can, and does, affect the supply and, therefore, the price. Over the past half century, the steel industry (steel corporations act in unison) has operated at production rates varying from 15% of capacity to 100% of capacity. You see, the supply of steel is limited to that which can be priced to yield the desired profit, without much regard to operating efficiency. Obviously operation way below capacity is less efficient than at some rate nearer capacity. In other words, big business limits output to suit price conditions, not operating efficiency, and this limitation of supply smacks of monopoly.

A third monopolistic trait of big business, oddly enough, is the practice of advertising. It might seem that the competitive posture of the big advertisers as far as their advertising is concerned, is proof that competition rules the day. Not so. Under conditions of competition it is presumed that each seller turns out his goods at the least cost to himself. That is, you don't catch Farmer Jones adding to his potato production costs by advertising them on television. But the Jones Soup Corporation might spend more for advertising than for shipping the soup to market. The cost of advertising cannot be explained if competition, as the term applies in economics, is assumed. Advertising costs are explained by the theory of monopolistic competition. What it amounts to is this: the price is non-competitive but the few sellers compete for a larger share of *those buyers who will pay that price*. The price is monopolistic; the supply is monopolistic; only the advertising is competitive.

Private competitive enterprise as a complete economic system is an idea, a dream, a theory. As such, it seems almost perfect. Big business is a fact—an institution of men which is, therefore, imperfect. Any comparison of things as they are with things as they ought to be puts reality in a bad light. Monopolistic enterprise seems almost sinister when compared with the picture of theoretical perfection painted by the classical economists. But the trouble with the classical theories is this: maximum profits and minimum costs are not *necessarily* associated. The maximum possible profit is that which derives from monopoly price. Therefore, a free enterprise system *always* will be tending toward monopoly, and away from the perfection dreamed of by Adam Smith. That is, the profit motive inspires enterprisers to strive to gain monopoly status and monopoly price.

We have seen that this tendency as it operates on the ownership of farmland produces results that are dangerous to all of us, and that private competitive enterprise farming must be restored by governmental action. We have seen that monopoly price must inevitably occur as natural resources are depleted (as the supply becomes limited). So, nature's goods dare not be left in private hands at all. But it does not necessarily follow that all big business is bad. On the contrary, modern American mass-production industry, when it is operating full steam, is a marvel of applied engineering and managerial skill of a high order. Even if our biggest steel corporation was operating at 40% capacity because of depression conditions, there would be no reason to believe that this 40% could be produced better under some other type of ownership. The trouble would lie not in the way the 40% is produced, but in the 40% rate itself. But the Composite Economy proposes to eliminate depression conditions through the insurance technique, and to give some stability to prices. Under these conditions the mass-production industries should operate more efficiently and more to our satisfaction than in the present economy.

The tendency toward monopoly price, however, will persist. That is, big business under the Composite Economy will be big business still. True, certain monopolistic malpractices will be mitigated by price and production stability. But since there still will be few sellers for many buyers (and, of course, advertising) prices will be monopolistic, not competitive. As said before, so long as there is private enterprise there will be the tendency toward monopoly. But we are committed to private enterprise much the same as we are committed to the English language: for better or worse.

Under the Composite Economy, then, the efficiency of big business is expected to be improved; non-competitive prices and advertising are to be tolerated. But what about the misuse of economic power? True, if there is monopolistic enterprise there will be some misuse of power. It is not possible to predict how bad it will be under the new economy. But there are social forces at work now, and there will be then, that tend to oppose the misuse of economic power. Big labor unions tend to balance their power against that of the big corporations. In fact, big labor is the social response to the challenge of big business. Other groups such as farmers tend to use their political advantage of numbers to get benefits that tend to offset their economic disadvantage. For example, the farmers of one Iowa county could outvote the whole theater-full of corporation presidents. Of course, this use of political power to counteract economic power leads to what has been called the "balance of abuses" and is not a final answer to the problem. But there are *no purely economic forces* that would tend to prevent excessive economic power, or the misuse of it. So, obviously, other social forces must be used. In a profit economy the economic forces at work are pushing *toward* monopoly. If this trend is to be resisted, other social forces must be used to oppose it or regulate it.

The effectiveness and worth of this "balance of abuses" are still matters for debate among economists. The term "balance of abuses" was used by the New Deal liberals to indicate their disfavor. Earlier Thorstein Veblen had scornfully labeled the same thing "concessive mitigation." More recently Professor Galbraith of Harvard used the term "countervailing power" and argued that it was reasonably acceptable. The point is that monopolistic enterprise, considering both its good points and its bad ones, is not intolerable now and might well improve under the Composite Economy. In any event there is no practicable alternative for monopolistic enterprise that could be blended in the non-revolutionary reforms required for the Composite Economy. Even so, this problem of power dare not long be left unsolved. A possible solution will be examined in the final chapter.

*　*　*

The Composite Economy, then, requires no revolutionary overturn, only reform. Indeed, in view of the serious nature of the problems we face, the number of necessary reforms is surprisingly small. They are as follows:

1. Land reform
2. The socialization of natural resources
3. Federal control over insurance companies
4. The socialization of savings
5. The elimination of existing debt
6. Bank reserve requirements raised to 50%

In addition to these, there is one preliminary reform: minimum production quotas for corporate food-processing industries. So, you see there are really only a half-dozen indispensable acts between us and the Composite Economy. Admittedly these reforms will require at least a moderate amount of legislation, some litigation, and a lot of bookkeeping. But it will prove better to sweat over ruled ledgers than weep over a disintegrating society.

10

CONCLUDING NOTES

> It is the condition of economic freedom that men
> should not be ruled by an authority which they cannot
> control.
>
> R. H. TAWNEY
> *The Acquisitive Society*

The Composite Economy, as outlined in the preceding memorandum, was devised to meet the minimum economic requirements. That is, it would work. Men would be employed steadily.
Basic foods would be produced dependably, and at competitive
prices. Natural resources would be conserved so as to be per-
manently available. Economic growth at the desired rate—even
when zero growth becomes necessary—would be automatically
provided for. The mass-production industries would operate
steadily. The achievements of such an economy would be as
necessary and important as the full market basket, though little
more magnificent.

Of course, the present American economy will not—cannot—
do these things. Either the market basket is stuffed overfull with
things that are owed for, or it is empty of bread—with a pronounced theoretical bias toward the latter. Worse yet, the
trouble with the present economy doesn't end there. Institutions
do not improve themselves: improvement comes only from the
people who operate them. As an institution, a profit economy is
a special kind of problem: if let alone, it will not simply stay the
same; it will get worse. The dream of Adam Smith notwithstand-
ing, the net effect of the economic forces in a profit economy pulls
it *away* from the social optimum—not toward it. So, other social
forces must be applied, constantly, merely to stand still.

The Composite Economy would be a better institution than the present one. But, it would not improve itself. So any improvement, as with the existing economy, must come by democratic process. This is not to say that the government ever must operate the economy; but the people, through democratic action, must see that the economy operates in accordance with their settled judgment.

In this chapter we will examine some glaring defects that will be present in the Composite Economy and suggest plausible means of improvement. These defects are not just loose ends left dangling by the preceding memorandum which, when tied up, will make the Composite Economy one neat package. Rather, they are serious complex defects present in the existing economy and will be carried over into the new one. They will not prevent the Composite Economy from working, but will prevent it from working well enough for those who want more than just economic efficiency. Besides, as with most defects in a profit economy, they will grow worse unless acted upon by the deliberately applied force of democratic action.

I. A NEW TYPE OF ANTITRUST POLICY

At long last, we shall now have a go at one uneconomic aspect of monopolistic price. This may seem a very modest aim. In a way it is. But monopolistic price bears about the same relationship to the growth toward monopoly as stagnant water bears to the growth of mosquitoes. If one didn't exist, neither would the other.

As a first approximation, think of monopolistic price as that price which produces the *desired* level of profit. With this in mind, it is understandable that all business enterprises, in a profit economy, strive for the power to command that price. Those that succeed wax fat and become fixtures in our industrial complex in, say, the oil, steel, auto, tobacco or breakfast food industries. Others succeed less well: so they continue striving, or merge with other firms or into conglomerates; or they find that they have achieved a satisfactory niche in the economy, considering the circumstances.

So, we can state, as a broad working definition, that monopolistic price is that price which produces a level of profit that is *satisfactory* to the businessman, everything considered. From this concept of monopolistic price we can proceed to develop a small improvement in our antitrust policy, even though we are dealing with a complex and constantly changing price system.

Earlier we took note of Adam Smith's pronouncement that competitive price was the lowest which could be taken; monopoly price the highest which could be got. Competitive price, which tends to equal marginal cost, prevails where there are many sellers and many buyers. Monopoly price occurs when there is only one seller. Between these two extremes lies the range of monopolistic prices which tend always to exceed marginal cost and, in general, apply when there are a *few* sellers for many buyers. It is in this broad range—limited by the abhorrence of free competition on the low side and the vague threat of the antitrust laws on the high side—where the bulk of American private enterprise operates and sets its prices. The method by which the prices are set is, conceptually at least, quite simple: it is accomplished merely by adding a markup to the unit cost.

In the present economy this monopolistic-price group of enterprises accounts for well over half of our national income. Being so large it embraces not only all of our largest corporations but many smaller ones too. Theoretically, these smaller units might be expected to offer enough competition to reduce the average markup a bit. Actually, however, they seldom do because of the uncertainty of what, in turn, the big boys might do to them. So the little firms follow the lead of the big ones.

Again, since this monopolistic group is so large it obviously includes both our very best companies and the very worst; both the efficient and the inefficient; some that are indispensable, some malevolent. But it must be understood that simply because a company holds a monopolistic position and the power to set its prices, this is not, in itself, proof that it maintains its favorable position other than by superior business efficiency.

However, the gain of monopolistic price through pervasive, or "national," advertising is something else again. "National" advertising[1] is, in itself, proof that profits are not maximized solely by business efficiency. The monopolistic price for a nationally advertised product obviously must include the usual costs of production and distribution, plus the desired profit markup, plus the cost of the mass advertising, *plus*. The last "plus" is simply another markup. Monopolistic enterprise would not incur the costs of advertising unless it paid back to them *more* than the costs. The saying "it pays to advertise" is quite accurate as it applies to the advertiser. But what it pays him, together with what it costs him, must be paid by the consumer.

At present, we tolerate this cost-of-advertising-plus fairly well. In any event, we accept it. Of course we once accepted raw milk and unfiltered water, too, until we learned how dangerous these things were, and how easy it was to correct them. On the other hand one noted economist argued that any savings resulting from the abatement of advertising likely would be transferred to some equally useless purpose; and that liquor advertising, for example, serves hardly less social purpose than the liquor itself. But this latter argument would lose its punch if "liquor" was replaced by "bread."

Let us assume, for the moment, that mass advertising by the monopolists has been drastically reduced. Let us grant that those who sang commercials have transferred to nightclubs, and that the lumber for billboards is being used, instead, for racetrack grandstands. Even so, won't good liquor efficiently produced supersede the brands that were merely well advertised? Won't the efficient producer of good soap gain the reward previously reaped by the blatant advertiser? And the same with bread and soup? Besides, if it turns out that the corporate giant was indeed holding its favorable position mainly through the incessant use of psychological persuasion (pervasive advertising), won't there be an emergence of smaller, more efficient firms? In other words,

---

[1]This does not refer to local retailers who hawk their wares by advertising in newspapers, radio, TV, etc., to attract customers. This refers, rather, to large manufacturers creating the image of the "nationally advertised product."

bereft of its psychological advantage, the monopolistic producer would have to compete for its share of the market on *economic* grounds. Then we would soon learn whether a company was big because it was efficient in the art of production, or in the art of spoofing. If the former—and in many cases it will so turn out— it will hold its monopolistic advantage. Although the monopolistic price would not be quite so high (due to the absence of adver- tising-costs-plus), it still would be monopolistic price. However, if the monopolist was only spoofing, there would be encourage- ment and room for the entrance of competitive enterprise.

So you see, mass advertising involves much more than just the cost-of-advertising-plus. It involves more than merely the waste of the ad men, the paper, ink and billboard lumber; more even, than the excessive price of the product. *It also involves both the quality of the product and the quality of the producer.* In many cases, it involves the *size* of the producer, too. Under the cover of uneconomic advertising may be hidden inferior products, inefficient producers—and bigness that is too big.

It is doubtful, of course, that the big mass-production in- dustries will suffer any great change in the absence of pervasive advertising. Steel beams, motorcars, airliners and steam turbines no doubt will be made by giant corporations for many years to come. But perhaps one day bread again will be baked in local bakeries instead of manufactured in giant factories; naturally aged flour stone-ground in local mills by private competitive enterprisers; and competitive production of butter and cheese, and soap and soup, and maybe even booze and cigarettes.

How can we achieve an economy free from monopolistic ad- vertising and, therefore, one in which competitive enterprise might grow and thrive? Quite easily. At present, monopolistic corporations are taxed at a rate of about 50% on net income. But all of their advertising costs are tax deductible. For retail outlets like Macy's, Sears and the A & P, the cost of advertising *is* legitimate since they must hawk their wares. But the *manu- facturers* have no economic justification to charge the consumer for subjecting him to psychological persuasion. So, if the cost of advertising aimed at the consumer (except by the retailers) was

not deductible from their corporate income tax, we might soon
find out which were the spoofers. And learn, at last, how big is
too big.

II. A CORPORATE CONSCIENCE

Monopolistic enterprise—cured of its manic-depressive tendencies, precluded from producing uneconomic pecuniary accumulations, forbidden the misuse of arable land and the destruction of natural resources, and dissuaded under pain of
taxation from waging psychological warfare against the people—
will be big business still. Those corporations that remain—and
there will be many—should be the stronger for the process. The
speculators, the spongers, the spoilers and the spoofers will be
weeded out. The remaining corporations will remain because
they produce superior products—whether tin cans or airliners—
in a superior manner. A manner, that is, superior in performance.

But superior performance, in itself, does not imply the social
optimum. Society demands, too, satisfactory answers to the questions "For what purpose?" and "By what means?" Too often we
have seen that another goal, hidden behind the profit motive, is
power. Power to sway political and judicial decisions, power to
propagandize, power over the lives and livelihoods of others.
Further, with respect to the giant corporations, too often have
we seen that the means itself is heavily weighted with use of
power.

In the Composite Economy, this problem of the misuse of
economic power has been left in the hands of those who will
fight against it. Through the balance of abuses, or countervailing
power, the force of the economic giant is to be balanced, or
countered, by the response of those against whom the force is
applied.

Incidentally, this social force on which we are relying is
really nothing more than *the right to fight back:* by labor unions,
the farm bloc, consumer cooperatives, or any other social, political
or economic combination that is strong enough to make the fight.
That, in fact, there is such a force is not open to serious question.

It is quite obvious that the scissors problem of the 1920s and early 1930s gave birth to the congressional "farm bloc" that fought for the farmers' interests, and that the labor practices of the big steel corporations during the early decades of the century provided the necessity for the United Steel Workers Union which is much in evidence today.

As for the alleged social efficiency of this countervailing force, however, there is much doubt. Perhaps if there is any typical trait to be found in the pattern of those cases where the abuse of economic power by monopolistic enterprise has, in fact, been countered by those who were abused, it is one of slow and painful process. The CIO is not the child merely of the 72-hour week, but also of the Homestead strike and the battle of the overpass at River Rouge. And the farmers paid for their government subsidies with three million foreclosures. There may come, at long last, a balance of power. But there is no redress for the pain and sacrifice, or the blood that was spilled, in the struggle to gain that balance.

Such a grim and cumbrous social process is clearly unfit for a civilized society.

Actually, this whole melancholy struggle against the misuse of economic power is the result of a tragic oversight. A corporation, you see, is a creature of the State. In a democracy the State is a creature of the people. Perhaps not once has it occurred to an ousted worker, or a dispossessed farmer, that the oppressive corporate power arrayed against him was a *thing created in his own name as a citizen:* a legal, privileged, corporate entity chartered by the State, endowed with power—but lacking a conscience. Surely, never knowingly would the citizens of a democratic society create a power that they could not control.

What has been overlooked is the corporate charter. The State—the people, that is—grants a charter to a business firm. It thereby endows this firm with the legal personality we call "incorporation." In this charter, the State—the people—sets forth the conditions under which the corporation must operate, and the limits of its rights. If this publicly granted corporate charter were to require that at least one-third of the directors be elected

by the employees to protect their rights, and at least one other
director be appointed by the State to represent the public at
large, perhaps this soulless corporation could be endowed with
some humanity. By political action this could be accomplished.
State charters of interstate corporations would be called up; new
charters would be granted by the federal government. Intrastate
corporation charters would be revised by the States.

Some might shudder at the thought of requiring corporations
to accept public and labor representatives on their governing
boards. But the most competent of our great industries well
might welcome so benign an intrusion. In the main, our modern
corporate giants are quite proud of their efficiency, technical
virtuosity and ability to improve. Conversely they are probably
secretly ashamed of their antidemocratic, antipublic and antilabor
practices and would be willing to change under a system that
saw that all the others would change too.

III. TRANSCENDENCE THROUGH REFORM

Over the pages we have examined the existing economy in
a critical way. We have found it to be motivated by greed,
mathematically improbable, hideously destructive, inhumane and,
in some aspects, downright absurd. Worse yet, in the few remaining pages we will briefly examine two more defects that are
as horrifying, each in its own peculiar way, as any previously
examined.

In view of all these terrible defects in the economy, one might
easily jump to the conclusion that it is not worth saving. A
poultryman facing bankruptcy simply because he produced an
abundance of chickens and eggs well might decide that the
existing economy is not worth a damn. Orderly-minded folks—
mathematicians, engineers and the like—might consider that the
system's failure to generate effectual purchasing power equal to
the price of the stuff produced proves it totally worthless. Sensi-
tive people mourning the destruction of nature's living things,
its landscapes and streams—all for the sake of profit—must, in
conscience, feel bitterness toward the profit economy. In each of

these cases, the opinion reached is justified and reasonable *as first thought*. However, so important a matter must be given second thought.

If the existing economy is evil and worthless beyond all redeeming it, what then shall we put in its place? Would we put our hard-pressed farmers on communal farms? Put the United Auto Workers under a commissar? Place our transportation and steel industries under the British socialist-type of bumbling direction? Certainly these questions answer themselves. It is doubtful whether communism, socialism and fascism have in them anything for us except the lessons of their failures.

Of course, few of us have firsthand knowledge of the inadequacies of these other systems. But millions of Americans have had experience with our military services. Many of the aspects of fascism, communism and socialism are to be found there: the authoritarianism, the inefficiency, the bumbling. For those who have served in the military, this reminder will be enough. Most others will readily recognize the likelihood of habitual inefficiency in institutions that are not bound by the economic discipline associated with private enterprise and private property. True, as *military* organizations, our professional army, navy and air force are the equal of any in the world. When expanded by the influx of civilians conditioned by the private economy and equipped with the products of American private industry, they have proved better than any in the world. There's the lesson. Socialism, communism, fascism or some mixture thereof, can be acceptable as a way of operating a *military* system. Such a system need not produce, nor please the people nor supply their material needs. *Our* economic system must do these things and, moreover, ours should measure up to American ideals. The answer, of course, is to reform the existing economy, not try to supplant it with any of those systems already proved historically as unfit for import.

That reform is the right answer will now be supported by two impressive examples. There are two nasty defects in the existing economy not previously expounded. Both are sore spots of long standing. That is, they have been well publicized in many books and are widely discussed. Embarrassingly so, for one makes us the subject of ridicule; the other, of hatred, fear and distrust. The former goes by the name *Inflation;* the latter is called *Imperialism.* Both will be so mitigated by the Composite Economy that a little more reform might render them harmless.

INFLATION

For more than a hundred and fifty years, the social desirability of *laissez-faire* capitalism was protected from destructive criticism by a beautiful edifice of theory. But this edifice, called "classical economics," was erected on a vulnerable foundation: assumption. First, it was assumed that full employment was the *normal* condition. Surely everyone who wanted to consume would first have to work at the process of production. Surely there would be a place for him on the production lines, since any act of production created total income exactly equal to the price of the output. These assumptions were so neat and pretty, that when contradictory facts arose they were brushed off.

Confidently, the theorists built on this neat foundation. Wages and prices, they argued, should stay stable because total income and total price were equal, and increasing production would permit population growth, thus providing more workers. Normal thrift would automatically assure that enough production would be saved (not consumed) to provide the desired amount of investment.

Now let us see what we have. First, everybody who wants a job can get one. Production is always at the optimum. Wages and prices are steady. If consumption is high (say 95% of the total product), then investment will be low (5%). But if consumption is frugal (say 50%), then investment will be high (50%). This, one modern critic jibed, is the logic of the insane. If only 50% of current capacity is being consumed, why would anyone invest in more production facilities? And when 95% of current capacity is "sold out" why should investment practically cease?

So, the "classical" theory conflicts with reality. If consumption is high—as indeed it would be at full employment—then obviously it would be profitable to build new factories. But, with everyone already employed, one would have to hire workers away from their current jobs to get them to build the new factories. Even in the days before unions, this meant offering higher wages to get the workers to shift jobs. With this done, production of goods declines (since some workers have stopped making goods in order to build new factories). But the demand for goods has increased: the building of new factories consumes some of the materials being made by the existing factories; and the shifted workers have more wages to spend. So prices rise, and all the forces involved continue to push them higher.

Alas, full employment is not the "normal" state of a free economy; rather it is the point where price inflation takes off into the wild blue yonder. The ridiculous part of the whole business is that price inflation actually sets in every time our economy even approaches its full production potential.

Being so highly vulnerable to ridicule on this score, we cannot escape it. But we can, for the while, endure it. You see, there is another side of the coin. Generally our economy operates *below* capacity, and price inflation has occurred in only about 30 years of the past 150 (one year in five, that is). Most of the time, not price inflation, but unemployment and depression are the problems. And these are problems the Composite Economy is designed to solve. But note this: despite all the ridicule about our price inflation whenever our economy gets near to full output, it generally escapes this by operating *below* maximum. Even then it often outperforms the ism-economies of Russia, England, etc.

With the inception of the Composite Economy, new factors will bear against our economy's susceptibility to price inflation. First will be the precise central control over the money supply. Second will be the curtailment of credit and the impossibility of credit binges. Further, the investment activity of the insurance technique can be operated very precisely against the cycle—either deflation or inflation. True, when price inflation threatens, investment must be slowed down, thereby *creating* some relative unemployment. But this could be done carefully, selectively and promptly. How well this will work and how satisfactory it will be must be learned by experience. Deliberately creating some unemployment (relative, of course; that is, 35 hours per week instead of 40) appears open to criticism. But it is more sensible than the present economy's mad impulse to increase investment at full employment, and decrease investment when employment decreases. It well may be that there *is* a price to pay for the privilege of maintaining a private enterprise profit economy in the face of a powerful economic law that says you can't. But the Composite Economy will reduce that price.

Another factor, hitherto nonexistent, could be the employee representation on the boards of directors (the corporate conscience). Being privy to the corporation's financial figures, the employees will know what productivity increase should accrue to them as increased wages. Further, the employees' directors will tend to restrain price increases—the workers lose, not gain, from increased prices. But here, too,—if it works—there may be a price to pay. Soon, the UAW members at General Motors would be paid better than the UAW members at Bumble Motors. Then, the better workmen would gravitate toward the better pay to the further disadvantage of Bumble Motors.

Even so, the Composite Economy will put new weight on the scales against our inherent price instability. Some new experience, some more study, then some more reform, and someday we will achieve a steady-state dollar.

IMPERIALISM

We will now consider the most damaging charge ever made against our present type of economic system: Imperialism! Briefly, the argument runs as follows. No matter how you look at it, the capitalist system is producing a surplus for the owners of capital. At first, it is a surplus of goods. An owner pays out $9 million to produce goods priced at $10 million. After the generated purchasing power is spent, the owner has a million dollars worth of goods left to do with as he wishes. If he sells the goods he will have a million dollars to do with as he wishes. So, he has either more goods than he can consume, or more funds than he can spend, or a mix of both.

There is a problem associated with profitable disposal of either surplus on a strictly internal basis. It can be difficult to sell the goods internally since the purchase price must be provided by credit, public or private. If the surplus goods are sold internally, sluggishly and with difficulty, it becomes apparent that the surplus funds should not be reinvested. Plant expansion would only mean a bigger surplus of goods to try to sell on a resistant market. There is, therefore, an internally produced pressure on the owner of capital impelling him to seek external markets for his surplus goods or external investment opportunity for his surplus funds.

When he peddles his goods overseas, or invests his surplus funds there, he finds he has competition. The French are here, the Dutch there and the British everywhere. Now, like the relationship between nature and the vacuum, the profit system abhors competition. So the markets are divided among the capitalist nations. Boundaries are established. Armies and navies are enlarged to protect them: and we have colonialism. England acquires India. Holland acquires South Africa. Belgium, Germany, England, Italy and France divide up the rest of Africa. Then the fighting starts and we have *Imperialism:* England wrests South Africa from the Dutch; Germany makes a grab and loses her overseas colonies to the competition; Italy grabs for more of Africa; Japan grabs the Philippines from America; America takes them back.

For a hundred years, history seemed to have little to do but pile up evidence in support of the charge of imperialism. Actually, imperialism fed on itself. The ever-growing military establishments, in addition to protecting and expanding the markets overseas, provided more internal markets and profitable outlets for investment plus jobs for the unemployed. Further, the recurrent warfare produced a political climate highly unfavorable to social or economic reform at home or in the colonies.

The profit system survived the charge that inflation would

cause it to self-destruct. But the charge of imperialism was more serious: the drive for profits was cause for destroying somebody else. This idea spread throughout the world. It fostered hatred and distrust, widespread and persistent. From it the British now have retreated. Both their old empire and their capitalist economy have been largely abandoned. And so it is with the French, the Belgians, the Italians and the Dutch.

You may read the evidence of history to suit your personal taste. We all read it with some bias. We may concede that the British were truly guilty, and so were some of the others. But America, we say, was not imperialistic. Besides, the almost perfect meshing of history and the theory of imperialism may be only a coincidence. Unfortunately, however you read the writing in the books, the writing on the wall says: "American, go home." There's the crux. On the charge of imperialism it doesn't matter what we think. It matters what *they* think. And they think we drop the bombs for the profit of it.

The best way to escape the assignment of guilt is to be above suspicion. You will note that the Composite Economy provides an internal market for all goods and provides an outlet for investment. There will be, therefore—and this is important—*no national economic need* for any imperialistic activity whatever. This is a big step in the height we must climb to rise above suspicion. You see, the rest of the world believes the theory that we drop the bombs for the profit of it. The Composite Economy carries within itself theoretical proof of the *absence* of a national profit motive for armaments, or foreign markets, or war. So, if *then* we should bomb Cambodia, it would mean that we were trying to *kill Cambodians,* not just making prosperity for Americans. There is a nice transcendence here if you can see it.

Look at it this way. The Composite Economy will not eliminate the profit on a bomb. But it will make possible an equal profit if the bomb ingredients are used instead for fertilizer and auto parts. Under the insurance technique, our government could get all the bombs it wants rental-applied to purchase price. That is we *could* bomb now and pay later—without interest charges.

But each bomb dropped would be a net *loss* to the national wealth; there can be no net gain since all the labor and materials in the bombs *would* (not just could) have been used for making internal wealth.

The Composite Economy has another theoretical advantage in this matter. Our detractors point to our exploitation of foreign resources as an example of imperialism. No one denies, or could, that we are net importers of iron ore, pulpwood, petroleum and many nonferrous metal ores because we squandered our own. Our detractors will add that profits were made in the squandering and more profits will be made as we squander the resources of others. That is the charge; it cannot be disproved. But, with the socialization of our natural resources a new principle appears. Of the living things, we will harvest no more than the sustained yield; of the others, we will have a perpetual supply. Of some we could use more and will pay fair value to those who want to sell. But, in principle, we could get along forever on what we have. That's enough to contradict the rationale that supports the accusation of exploitation.

Wars have causes other than the profit motive. But the *idea* that capitalism *must* exploit and expand and wage war for profit arose from the defects in unreformed profit economies. It was a simple idea with a simple theory and it swept the world. It caused more mischief, at least to us, than did imperialism itself. It will continue to plague us so long as it remains so believable. And yet the nonrevolutionary reforms of the Composite Economy would cut the theoretical basis for the idea right out from under it. Without this basis, the idea itself must weaken. Eventually, it could wither and die.

Not, however, without further reforms. Someday an international currency must supplant the Yankee dollar. Someday international trading accounts should be multilaterally balanced so that each country gives as good as it gets and vice versa. But before we can help to reform the world we have much to reform at home. Reform is something we should have a good supply of for ourselves before we try to export any.

IV. THE POSSIBILITY AND THE IDEA
OF THE COMPOSITE ECONOMY

Even upon reading to this point some may question: (1) Isn't this New Economy really out of reach? and (2) Isn't the *idea* of it really out of this world? Of course, the best way not to succeed is, for whatever reason, not to try. So let us consider each question briefly, even though the answers will require of intelligent skeptics further thought and an additional reading assignment.

1. On the Possibility

In principle, the New Economy is attainable given our existing political capabilities. The early, urgent reforms of the New Deal were carried out in the first hundred days. The six basic reforms required to bring the Composite Economy into being might be accomplished in an orderly way within, say, four years, provided the conditions are favorable.

In practice, however, conditions are seldom favorable. One harsh, but reasonably expectable, set of circumstances might well be as follows. As the old economy begins to collapse, the vested interests will resist reform, using all their financial and political power to retain their privileges and authority. Finally the dam will break: bankruptcies and unemployment will surge; financial panic will ensue. There is chaos, and revolution becomes a real threat. In the face of such an explosive social challenge could the ideas of the Composite Economy furnish the basis for quick response?

Yes. Recall that the banking system in the New Economy is to hold currency reserves in its vaults of 50% of total deposits. As of 1976 total deposits amount to about $800 billion. Vault reserves therefore should be $400 billion. Now, to maintain the existing deposits and move toward the new reserve total, the central monetary authority would have a one-time pump-priming capability of up to $400 billion. As this new currency is issued (faster or slower as the state of the panic requires) it will be used first to pay wages for new employment. But as the new currency enters the banks, mainly for the repayment of bank loans, it would be sequestered in the vaults until the 50% reserve requirement is reached.

When the crisis is over both the amount of bank deposits (including checkbook money) and the currency in circulation would stand at about the same level as before the economic collapse began. Only the bank reserves would have increased, and bank loans (debt) would have decreased. With the panic over, the remaining reforms to establish the New Economy could be put in place in an orderly way.

2. On the Idea

The socialization of natural resources is now so commonplace it is no longer an idea: it is the practice. As each country becomes aware that American robber barons are stealing their resources the country simply organizes and takes over their birthright. Mexico, the Arab nations, most recently Venezuela are good examples. While we as a nation are not yet aware that our robber barons are destroying our future, the *idea* of socialization is surely not OTW.

Land reform is both ubiquitous and ageless. Every country in the world did—or, one day, must—undertake land reform. This, too, is no longer an idea; it is an inevitability. Nothing out of this world about land reform.

This leaves the idea of the insurance technique (including the socialization of savings and the transformation of debt) as the only one to startle or arouse suspicion. To allay this I can offer no better answer than a reading assignment: Chapter 24 of *The General Theory of Employment, Interest and Money* by John Maynard Keynes. It is titled "Concluding Notes on the Social Philosophy towards which the General Theory might lead."

Reading this final chapter in Keynes's towering work will enlighten you on two contrasting things. First, you will come to realize that the economists who manipulated the existing economy from Truman's time through Nixon's and Ford's did *not* pursue the social philosophy Keynes had outlined for them. They were merely *political* economists doing what the dominant political establishment wanted them to do. Second, it will inform you that the growth of wealth is *impeded* by the rich; that the functionless investor deserves no bonus; that interest rewards no genuine sacrifice; that investment is promoted by a *low* interest rate and that banking policy is unlikely to sufficiently lower the rate; that the world will not much longer tolerate the inevitable unemployment associated with capitalism. So, you see, the idea of the insurance technique is neither otherworldly nor without precedent.

❋   ❋   ❋

One thing in the Composite Economy will be new: its underlying motivation. Our present economy is motivated mainly by greed. Communism operates on terror; except in the Maoist variant the terror is tempered with propaganda. Socialism, it seems, is inspired mainly by *hope*. The Composite Economy, however, will be motivated by mankind's desire for security.